NECK

Very strong, muscular, almost cylindrical. Enormous neck with ample skin, loose and supple. Average circumference equals almost that of the head. The dewlap, well defined, starts at the level of the throat and forms folds to the chest.

TAIL

Very thick at the base. The tip does not reach below the hock. Carried low, deeply set. Hanging when at rest, generally raised from 90—120° in relation to this vertical position when the dog is active.

FOREQUARTERS

Strong bone structure, legs very muscular. Elbows neither turned in nor out too much. Forearm is straight or slightly inclined inward in order to get closer to the medium plane, especially with very broad chests. Pasterns are powerful, slightly sloping, sometimes a little turned. Feet are strong and tight. Nails curved preferably pigmented. Pads well developed and supple.

BODY

Chest is powerful, well ribbed up, broad, let down deeper than the elbows. Powerful forechest. Sternal ribs rounded. Other ribs well sprung and well let down. The circumference of the chest must be 0.25—0.30 metres (10—12 inches) superior to the height at the withers.

COAT

Fine hair which is short and soft to the touch.

COLOUR

Reddish brown, the colour of mahogany or in the range of the fawn shades. Good pigmentation is desirable. Small white patches on the chest and feet are allowed.

HINDQUARTERS

Thighs are well developed and thick, muscles visible. Stifle in parallel plane to the vertical median plane or slightly turned inward or outward. Lower thigh is relatively short, muscular and well let down. Hock is short and sinewy with the angle of the hock relatively open. When viewed from the rear, the parallel hind legs give the impression of power, although the hindquarters are slightly less broad than the forequarters.

SIZE

Between 45—50 kgs (100—110 lbs). Bitches lighter than dogs. Males 60—68 cms in height at the withers; females 58—66 cms at the withers (23—26 ins). Size should be in proportion to the size of the head.

Dogue de Bordeaux

by Joseph Janish

Table of Contents

9

25

History of the Dogue de Bordeaux

Learn about the ancient beginnings of this rare French Mastiff and the evolution of this multi-talented guard dog, hunter and warrior. Follow the Dogue de Bordeaux around the world and see its influence on other breeds and cultures.

35

Characteristics of the Dogue de Bordeaux

Meet a charming, friendly canine in a muscular 45-kg package: the Dogue de Bordeaux can make an ideal companion and protector for the right owner, home and family. Understand the unique physical, temperamental, and breed-specific health concerns.

44

The Breed Standard of the Dogue de Bordeaux

Learn the requirements of a well-bred Dogue de Bordeaux by studying the description of the breed set forth in the breed standard. Both show dogs and pets must possess key characteristics as outlined in the breed standard.

72

Your Puppy Dogue de Bordeaux

Be advised about choosing a reputable breeder and selecting a healthy puppy. Understand the responsibilities of ownership, including home preparation, acclimatization, the vet and prevention of common problems.

DISTRIBUTED BY:

INTERPET
PUBLISHING

Vincent Lane, Dorking
Surrey RH4 3YX England

Copyright © 2001 Animalia Books S. L.
SECOND EDITION:
Copyright © 2003 by Animalia Books S. L.
Cover design patent: US 6,435,559 B2
Printed in South Korea.

Everyday Care of Your Dogue de Bordeaux

Enter into a sensible discussion of dietary and feeding considerations, exercise, grooming, travelling and identification of your dog. This chapter discusses Dogue de Bordeaux care for all stages of development.

88

Housebreaking and Training Your Dogue de Bordeaux

by Charlotte Schwartz
Be informed about the importance of training your Dogue de Bordeaux, from the basics of housebreaking, and understanding the development of a young dog, to executing obedience commands (sit, stay, down, etc.).

Photo Credits:

Norvia Behling
Carolina Biological Supply
Doskocil
Fleabusters, Rx for Fleas
Isabelle Francais
James E. Hayden, RBP
James Hayden-Yoav
Carol Ann Johnson

Dwight R. Kuhn
Dr. Dennis Kunkel
Mikki Pet Products
Jean Claude Revy
Spielman
Alice van Kempen
C. James Webb

Illustrations by Renée Low

144

Your Senior Dogue de Bordeaux

Recognise the signs of an ageing dog, both behavioural and medical; implement a senior-care programme with your veterinary surgeon and become comfortable with making the final decisions and arrangements for your senior Dogue de Bordeaux.

113

Health Care of Your Dogue de Bordeaux

Discover how to select a proper veterinary surgeon and care for your dog at all stages of life. Topics include vaccination scheduling, skin problems, dealing with external and internal parasites and the medical conditions common to the breed.

151

Showing Your Dogue de Bordeaux

Experience the dog show world, including different types of shows and the making up of a champion. Go beyond the conformation ring to working trials, field and agility trials, etc.

HISTORY OF THE

Dogue de Bordeaux

INTRODUCTION

Characterised by the largest, most magnificent head in dogdom and layered wrinkles on its face and hefty exaggerated paws, the Dogue de Bordeaux trudges into the hearts of people throughout the world. Originally used for cattle droving and guarding the vineyards in Bordeaux, this pugnacious, pug-faced French warrior has survived within a hair of its extinction through one national revolution, two World Wars, and a Hollywood adventure *Turner and Hooch*.

Sometimes referred to as the French Mastiff, Bordeaux Bulldog or simply 'DDB', the Dogue de Bordeaux has had an interesting background and development through the last five centuries. An extremely cooperative, intelligent, and fearless giant, the Dogue de Bordeaux has persisted in various vocations throughout the centuries, a testament to the breed's versatility and adaptability. Since the 1400s, the Dogue de Bordeaux has had many jobs: herding cattle, flock guarding, hunting ferocious game, animal baiting, dog fighting and film

Dogues de Bordeaux have a long history of being guard dogs. Their impressive stature alone is enough to frighten potential thieves.

(FACING PAGE) The Dogue de Bordeaux is often called the French Mastiff or Bordeaux Bulldog. One may recognise the Dogue as the star of the Hollywood production *Turner and Hooch*, with human co-star Tom Hanks.

9

DID YOU KNOW?

Dogs and wolves are members of the genus *Canis*. Wolves are known scientifically as *Canis lupus* while dogs are known as *Canis domesticus*. Dogs and wolves are known to interbreed. The term canine derives from the Latin derived word *Canis*. The term dog has no scientific basis but has been used for thousands of years. The origin of the word dog has never been authoritatively ascertained.

Bones of these big dogs have been found amongst other artefacts in archaeological expeditions throughout the world in places such as Tibet, China and India. These dogs were included in the army of Alexander the Great, and journeyed from Mesopotamia to Epirus in various wars. In Epirus there was a mythical king ruling over the area of Molossus who took care of the dogs. From there they journeyed to Rome, Gaule and other lands including Spain and France.

There are contrasting reports that this large dog first existed in Spain as the Alano, an extinct dog whose description resembles today's Dogue de Bordeaux. The Alano was supposedly brought to Europe by the Alans, an Oriental tribe. The Alan vautre was described in the fourteenth century by Gaston Phoebus (or Febus), Count of Foix, in his *Livre de Chasse*. 'He holds his bite stronger than three sight hounds'. There are also accounts that the molosser developed from the Molossids, a Greco-Roman canine that existed during Julius Caesar's time and was used in war.

acting. Powerful and surprisingly athletic, the Dogue de Bordeaux has never been intimidated and makes an excellent guardian. Beneath all that toughness, exists a sweet, sincere, slobberingly loveable character that makes a wonderful companion.

HISTORY AND BACKGROUND OF THE DOGUE DE BORDEAUX

The Dogue de Bordeaux falls into a group of dogs classified as molosser, descendants of the molossus, a dog that lived approximately 700 BC. Based on ancient carvings and paintings, it appears the molossus were kept as guard and hunting dogs by the Assyrians.

The first record of a molosser-type dog is in a letter dated 326 BC that mentions large, strong dogs with short, broad teeth.

DEVELOPMENT OF A DOGUE TYPE

The word 'dogue' first appeared at the end of the fourteenth century. Before the nineteenth century, these dogs did not have a standard but were very similar in looks and usage. There were

The Tibetan Mastiff joins the Dogue de Bordeaux in the group of dogs known as molossers. Tibetans have curved tails and long coats, in contrast to the hanging tails and short coats of the Dogue.

DID YOU KNOW?

Since dogs have been inbred for centuries, their physical and mental characteristics are constantly being changed to suit man's desires for hunting, retrieving, scenting, guarding, and warming their master's laps. During the past 150 years, dogs have been judged according to physical characteristics as well as functional abilities. Few breeds can boast a genuine balance between physique, working ability and temperament.

Tibetan Mastiff with puppy. Despite the shared ancestry, there is little resemblance to the Dogue.

guardian dogs used to protect homes, butcher shops, and vineyards; pack hunting dogs that baited bulls and pursued boars, bears, jaguars and other game; and herding dogs that took care of farm animals such as sheep and cattle. Eventually, the molosser developed into a variety of mastiffs including today's Tibetan Mastiff, Spanish Mastiff, Mastino Italiano (Neapolitan Mastiff), and Bullmastiff, to name a few.

One type of dog in France was called the Dogues or Doguin d'Aquitaine, a breed based on the French Molossus, which existed in the early fourteenth century and was bred for fighting other dogs, bears and boar. There were several variations of the Doguin d'Aquitaine, depending on the region and the jobs they needed to accomplish. As a result, their general appearance was inconsistent. There were various colours and varieties of coat, different jaw/bite patterns (undershot and overshot), and other slight variations. For the most part, however, these dogs were similar in body structure, weight and size. Eventually one type emerged as the preferred dog—the 'butcher's dog' that was used to protect meat shops and were highly coveted by the French noblemen and wealthy families as home guardians.

The first recorded reference to 'Dogue de Bordeaux' occurred in 1863 at the first canine exhibition at the Jardin d'Acclimatation in Paris, France. This was less a

The incorporation of the Dogue de Bordeaux into the Japanese Fighting Dog resulted in today's Tosa Inu.

12

conformation show than it was a catalogue of dog breeds. The winner of the exhibition was a bitch named Magentas who was identified according to the capital of its region of origin—thus, Dogue de Bordeaux.

Toward the end of the nineteenth century, the Dogue de Bordeaux travelled to England for fighting and show competition. In 1895 John Proctor published an article in the magazine *The Stock Keeper* describing his experience judging the 'fighting dogs of the South of France.' When English law made dog fighting illegal, the Dogue de Bordeaux was bred almost exclusively for conformation and temperament for competition in dog shows.

In 1896, veterinarian Pierre Meguin published the standard for the Dogue de Bordeaux in his magazine *L'Eleveur* (The Animal Breeder). He formalised a standard from a combination of the best Dogues de Bordeaux shown since Magentas captured top dog honours at Jardin d'Acclimatation. This standard was put forward by Meguin with a Mr Brooke, Dr Wiart and a group of French authorities. A year later, the standard was published in *The Breeds of Dog* by Henry de Bylants.

Until Meguin's standard, there was much controversy over the Dogue type, and diversity in breed type persisted. Head and body size fluctuated according to the particular breeder; both scissors and undershot bites were found; and the mask colour was extremely varied. During this time of uncertainty, there were at least three different styles of Dogue: the Toulouse, the Paris, and the Bordeaux. The Toulouse had a fawn or brindle coat of many colours, but otherwise was very similar to today's Dogue de Bordeaux. The Paris was also similar to the modern standard, but the bite varied with some having a scissors bite while others had a nearly one inch undershot. After much debate, the breeders decided upon today's undershot in the Dogue de Bordeaux standard.

In 1910, after three years of research, J Kunstler, a professor of comparative anatomy of the Science Facility of Bordeaux, wrote *Etude Critique du Dogue de Bordeaux*, a critical study of the breed that included a more precise standard than

Front view of the Tosa Inu. The word *inu* in Japanese means dog.

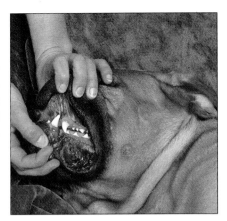

The undershot bite, where the lower jaw protrudes further than the upper jaw, is required according to the breed standard.

the original published by Meguin. Kunstler's standard is used to this day (albeit updated twice by Dr Raymond Triquet and Mr Tim Taylor), though there are some variations of the breed, identified as the Bordeaux type, the Paris type and the Mediterranean type. The differences between these types are slight and have mainly to do with the height and the head.

The breed standard evolved as interest in the Dogue de Bordeaux increased. The first standard ('*caractere des vrais dogues*') by Pierre Meguin appeared in *Le Dogue de Bordeaux* in 1896. The second standard was developed by J Kunstler and appeared in *Etude critique du Bordeaux* in 1910. The third standard was produced by Raymond Triquet, with the collaboration of Dr Maurice, a veterinarian, in 1971. The fourth standard was reformulated according to the Fédération

Cynologique Internationale's (FCI) Jerusalem model by breed expert Raymond Triquet, with the collaboration of Philippe Serouil, President of the French Dogue de Bordeaux Club, its club and committee in 1993.

EXPORTATION OF THE DOGUE
After the standard became known throughout the world, it was only a matter of time before the Dogue de Bordeaux was in demand for breeding programmes abroad. During the 1930s, the impressive size and character of the Dogue de Bordeaux attracted others to incorporate the breed into the Japanese Fighting Dog. Increasing the head and overall body size of Japan's Fighting Dog resulted in today's Tosa Inu. Similarly, the Martinez brothers of Argentina imported several Dogue de Bordeaux for infusion in their breeding programme. Their goal was a super dog that needed the Dogue's head size, overall size and strength, jaw strength, and courage. These same characteristics are essential elements of today's Dogo Argentino, the solid white creation of the Martinez brothers designed to pursue large game.

In the 1960s, Dr Philip Todd imported the Dogue de Bordeaux to the US, then moved with his Dogues to Holland, and introduced the breed to the Dutch.

The English Mastiff is another molosser 'cousin' of the Dogue de Bordeaux.

Toward the end of the 1960s, Dr Todd helped Steve and Wendy Norris establish a breeding programme in the US.

Throughout the world, the Dogue de Bordeaux is recognised by several canine organisations. The FCI, The Kennel Club (UK) and United Kennel Club (USA) are the most notable registries. The American Kennel Club (AKC), the largest canine registry in the US, still does not recognise the breed.

DOGUES AROUND THE WORLD
In the 1800s the breed was hardly known outside of his

The Boxer and the Dogue resemble each other in certain facial features.

native France although some exports took place to England as early as 1885 for the purpose of fighting and later for conformation shows. The first breeder of the Dogue in Scandinavia was H Kröller from Aalborg in Denmark in the beginning of the twentieth century.

UNITED KINGDOM

After five years of advocacy by the British Dogue de Bordeaux Club, The Kennel Club of Britain finally accepted the Dogue de Bordeaux in November of 1998. This move by The Kennel Club came just a few months after Raymond Triquet, known to many as 'The Father of the Dogue de Bordeaux', spoke at a seminar in Ascot. His presentation championing the breed was a key element in persuading The Kennel Club toward acceptance. The introduction of the breed was celebrated at a special exhibition of several Dogues de Bordeaux at Earls Court, the venue of the original Crufts event. Credit should also go to the most influential and supportive members of the British Dogue de Bordeaux Club including Ann Sutton, Karen Watson, Alan and Kerry Bates, and Paul and Karen Harris.

THE UNITED STATES

Introduced to the US in the 1960s by Dr Philip Todd and later campaigned by the hard-working Steve and Wendy Norris, the Dogue de Bordeaux found good friends in the US. The American dog world, however, had not grasped on to this quintessential French mastiff, and for the first twenty years, very few Dogues existed in the US and few if any serious fanciers committed themselves to the breed. By the 1980s, the Dogue de Bordeaux Club of America, dedicated to improving and importing quality specimens from Europe, made a great impact on the breed in America. The new parent club became well established with French breeders and experts, and only the finest Dogues made their way to America. More and more dog fanciers noticed the Dogue, and considerable interest was developing in the breed. In 1989 the breed gained in popularity after the release of the movie *Turner and Hooch*, starring Tom Hanks and featuring a well-trained, entertaining and attractive Dogue de Bordeaux. As the movie gained popularity, so did the breed—a double-edged sword for the Dogue de Bordeaux. It was good that North Americans were finally learning about this magnificent breed, but this surge in popularity

The Neapolitan Mastiff has a heavier head than the Dogue, yet it is still quite evident that the two breeds are related.

was unfortunately a bane for the breed. Too many profit-motivated, incompetent breeders quickly bred Dogues de Bordeaux that were not sound and did not conform to type. They bred Dogues with hip dysplasia or other known genetic maladies. Inbreeding was common and resulted in many Dogues with poor temperament and behavioural problems.

In the 1990s, several responsible Dogue de Bordeaux breeders have kept the proper Dogue type intact. The Dogue de Bordeaux Society has done an outstanding job of preserving type, and has established a rescue organisation that places

Nothing is as impressive as the head of the Dogue de Bordeaux, the grandest head in the dog world.

17

stray or abandoned Dogues de Bordeaux in adoptive homes that adhere to the organisation's code of ethics. The rescue organisation also will assist Bordeaux owners, who for any reason, can no longer provide a home for their dog.

The United States Bordeaux Corporation is a similar organisation with a specific code of ethics and the goal of betterment for the breed. Dogue de Bordeaux owners should also be familiar with the American Rare Breed Association (ARBA), a sponsor of several events that welcome the Dogue de Bordeaux.

Bye and bye, the Dogue de Bordeaux has a long way to go to become a popular pet or a household name. In the US, the breed is still regarded as a 'rare breed.' Although a dog show for rare breeds may attract as many as 25 quality Dogues de Bordeaux, this display in no way indicates that the breed is becoming as popular as the Great Dane or Bullmastiff, for example. Fortunately, there are many devoted breeders who will continue to promote the breed and establish an enthusiastic following in the States.

GERMANY

The Dogue de Bordeaux was introduced into Germany in the mid to late 1800s for many of the same reasons the breed found popularity in France. In Germany the Dogue de Bordeaux was a valuable working dog on farms, droving cattle and guarding flocks. Unrivalled as a protector and hunter, it was also used for hunting game and preventing wild boars from dismantling vineyards, farmland, and stock animals.

In 1908 a breed club was established for the Dogue de Bordeaux, the Allgemeiner Deutscher Bordeauxdoggen. After World War II this breed club was one of the founding members of the Verband fuer das Deutsche Hundewesen (VDH). Until 1978 this club was known under the name Club fuer Bordeauxdoggen und Mastiffs e.V. When the Mastino Napoletano, Bullmastiff, Fila Brasileiro, Tosa Inu and Spanish Mastiff joined the organisation, it was renamed Club fuer Molosser e.V. (Club for Molossian Breeds).

The breeds were under the supervision of several working groups (Arbeitsgemeinschaften = AG). Each breed has its own working group with one president who is elected by the group for two years.

SPAIN

Currently there are a few small bands of breeders who are developing excellent examples of the breed, and the Dogue is gaining popularity throughout the

Although the Dogue de Bordeaux should not look like an 'overgrown Bulldog,' there are evident similarities between the English Bulldog, shown here, and the Dogue. (Inset) A head study of the English Bulldog.

country. The breed has no specific national organisation but is recognised by the Club Español de los Molosos de Arena, a club for Molosser-type dogs that is similar to the German Club fuer Molosser e.V. Both the FCI and the Real Sociedad Canina sanction this club.

ITALY

The Dogue de Bordeaux is beginning to enjoy populari-ty throughout Italy. It has benefited from The Italian Club of Molosso (CIM), an organisation whose mission is to encourage, promote and educate breeders to preserve a superior strain in each of the following breeds: Bullmastiff, Dogue de Bordeaux, Dogo Argentino, Fila Brasileiro, Spanish Mastiff, Tibetan Mastiff, Pyrenean Mastiff and Tosa Inu. Their goal is to strengthen the selection of the Molossian breeds identified by the second group of the Italian Kennel Club (ENCI) that are not specifically represented or protected by another breeder's association.

CIM is an excellent organisation that publishes an informative newsletter *(I nostri cani)* and a quarterly bulletin. It also organises shows under the authority of, and in collaboration with, ENCI. CIM membership is open to Italian citizens as well as foreign-ers who agree to abide by the statutes, and whose application is accepted by the Council. Those interested in finding out more about the Dogue de Bordeaux in Italy should contact ENCI in Milan or CIM in Felino (Parma).

NETHERLANDS

In July 1975 the first litter of Dogues de Bordeaux was born in The Netherlands at the kennel of Mr Van den Doel in Berg en Dal. The only thing known about this litter is the NHSB (the Netherlands Dog Registry) registration.

Four years later the second litter was born, an 'A-litter' Dogues de Bordeaux 'Van de Ircomara', at the kennel of Mrs F. Schietekatte. The dam was a French import named Lia de Ker Saint Mesmes. The sire was Lex de la Berse du Loup from Germany. Development was slow and type inconsistent from there.

Dutch conformation shows have recently begun to include many Dogues de Bordeaux. The quality of the breed has improved drastically since the 1980s, and as a result, judging has been more consistent. Prior to the 1980s judges were simply looking for the good type, a common tactic with new breeds. Now that the ring participants are conforming to the accepted

There are clubs worldwide who are devoted to preserving type in molosser breeds such as the Dogo Argentino, shown here, and the Dogue de Bordeaux.

standard, judges can concentrate on the specifics such as finding the right balance between type and other qualities such as the body and the movement. Dutch breeders have succeeded fairly quickly in their objective of creating Dogues de Bordeaux with heavy bone, massive size, more wrinkles and fuller noses that compare favourably with the top Dogues in France. Judge Mr Bas Bosch N'Agor, who spent most of the 1980s studying the breed in France, has had a strong influence on the positive development of the Dogue de Bordeaux in The Netherlands.

Front view of the Dogo Argentino.

Support for the argument that the Dutch can breed great Dogues de Bordeaux came in 1994 when the bitch Nike de Legeane, bred by J Dijkstra and owned by Erik Planting, became World Champion. Also in 1994, the bitch Fitou Appelation Controlee, bred and owned by Erik Planting, was named Best Youth Bitch at the club match in Germany (UBX).

victories took place at the National d'Elevage in France where the male Mike, bred by F van Tuyl, became Best Youth Male, Lady Boss de la Maison de Hollande became Best Youth Bitch and Arlet van de Amilja, bred by J Bosma, became Best Bitch.

In spite of all these achievements, the Dutch continue to concentrate on conserving the

A Dogue male with his puppy. These are Dutch-bred dogs.

In 1996, the bitch Lady Boss de la Maison de Hollande, bred and owned by Gerard van 't Hul, tallied two youth titles: Youth World Champion and Youth Luxembourg Champion, and also won at the club match in Italy. Other Dutch Dogue de Bordeaux

athleticism, movement, personality and other qualities as well as keeping good type. The worst fear among breeders in The Netherlands is that the Dogue de Bordeaux will get too large, heavy and fat—characteristics that are equally despised in the rest of the world.

Much of The Netherlands' success can be attributed to Belmondo the Red Powerpack, a spectacular, dark red Dogue de Bordeaux that had great size and heavy bone yet retained the athleticism that is so desired in the breed. Belmondo was imported from Germany by Mrs Antonissen-van Strien. He was big and possessed wonderful bone; a massive, classic head with a perfect nose; a rare perfect topline and very strong forequarters and hindquarters. He was named 'Dog World's Top Dog of the Year 1992' in The Netherlands. His greatest foreign result was in 1994 when he gained Best Of Breed at the World Dog Show in Switzerland under the 'Father of the Dogue de Bordeaux' Raymond Triquet. Belmondo is credited with 18 litters between 1988 and 1997 that produced numerous champions. Before Belmondo, the most important Dogue was N'Agor de la Maison des Coqs x Lutteur du Gorge d'Or, who was the base of all breeding in Holland in the 1980s.

The Bullmastiff is a close relative of the Dogue who has gained much popularity as a pet. (Inset) A head study of the Bullmastiff.

23

CHARACTERISTICS OF THE
Dogue de Bordeaux

PHYSICAL CHARACTERISTICS OF THE DOGUE DE BORDEAUX

The Dogue de Bordeaux is a powerful, muscular dog that makes an excellent guard of both person and property. A compact, strongly built athlete, the Dogue possesses size that belies its agility and speed. These qualities were originally developed for working, protecting property, and hunting. As you study the Dogue's characteristics, keep in mind their original purposes.

The jaws are prominent due to strong development of the chewing muscle. This was a necessary characteristic for bull-baiting. The chest is very broad and the distance between the floor and the chest should be equal to or smaller than the back to the chest.The Dogue de Bordeaux should not look like an oversized Bulldog.

The coat is short, fine and silky, coloured in all shades of red and blonde to deep red mahogany. Good pigmentation of skin is favoured. White markings on the chest and feet are tolerated. The Dogue de Bordeaux should have a well-marked red or black facial mask. The colour of the nose corresponds to the mask.

TEMPERAMENT

Like all molossus-type dogs, the Dogue de Bordeaux has strong nerves and is not easily excited. Its personality is balanced, quiet and calm. Not very rowdy, it is rare to hear the Dogue de Bordeaux bark loudly without sufficient reason (i.e., an intruder entering the home). It is a very confident breed that does not need to prove itself to other dogs, unless it is challenged.

The Dogue de Bordeaux is a charming breed that is very warm and friendly to humans and small animals. It is a very good dog with children for two reasons. First, the Dogue de Bordeaux loves to be around humans—a family cannot be big enough. Second, the Dogue de Bordeaux has plenty of patience and will deal with the typical teasing, tail pulling, and other annoyances in which undisciplined children tend to engage. Dogues are happy to comply with the silliest of children's games, such as wearing hats and 'clothes.'

The Dogue de Bordeaux is intelligent, docile, and usually not inclined to fight. Male dogs tend to be more dominant and will occasionally fight with other

25

The impressive presence of a Dogue is a great deterrent to thieves. Despite his intimidating appearance, the Dogue is a charmer who loves to be with people, especially children. (Inset) Make no mistake—the Dogue is a formidable guard dog with the brawn to stand up to his bark.

The wrinkly faced Shar Pei bears some resemblance to the Dogue; the resemblance is even stronger between youngsters of the two breeds.

males to determine dominance. Dominance is an inherent trait of the Dogue de Bordeaux and must be accepted and dealt with by the Dogue owner.

Keep in mind that one of the original purposes of the Dogue de Bordeaux was to protect, which in many cases meant to fight. As a result, the Dogue de Bordeaux is aggressive by nature, will not back down from a fight (though it unlikely to instigate one), and will protect what is his own (and his owners). Proper socialisation of your Dogue is of the highest importance, and even well-socialised Dogues de Bordeaux must be monitored when in the presence of other dogs.

The Dogue de Bordeaux tends to be a very stubborn and arrogant breed, yet it is very trainable. Once the Dogue learns a command, he will never forget it. Because of his high intelligence, it is necessary to continue beyond basic obedience training. If you will not be using your Dogue de Bordeaux for hunting, trials, Schutzhund or other competition, then engage him in special tasks and jobs around the home. You will be surprised at how much your Dogue can learn and help with your everyday routine, and your pet will never be bored.

When training your Dogue de Bordeaux, always keep in mind this is a very self-confident,

arrogant, independent and stubborn breed. Thus, it makes no sense to scream, scold and shout like a drill sergeant. You will get much further by combining training with playtime—nothing is easier for a dog (and owner!) than learning by playing. You must use praise, rather than negativity, to train your Dogue de Bordeaux. Praise is the most important aid to education and will yield the quickest results. Praise everything your Dogue does correctly, from doing his duty outside to bringing in the newspaper.

Training your Dogue de Bordeaux requires patience, love and a well-filled bag of tricks to be successful. If the learning process is supported by pieces of meat, cheese or other delicacies, the Dogue de Bordeaux learns quickly. The smell of food has a magical way of eliminating the Dogue de Bordeaux's ego. Your most effective argument should be positive reinforcement—not physical clout. When necessary, the best reprimand is to shake the scruff of the neck.

Consistency is another essential element of successful training. If you cannot withstand the pleading look and allow your puppy to sit on the sofa, then it will soon be his sofa not yours! Letting the puppy sleep in bed and feeding him from the table are similar incidents. Keep in mind that the cute pug-faced puppy snuggling beside you will very shortly become a huge, heavy, slobbering 45-kgs dog that takes up the entire bed or sofa and is not inclined to move from his comfortable spot.

THE DOGUE DE BORDEAUX IN THE HOME

A willing worker who is happy to be around people and fairly cooperative, the Dogue de Bordeaux makes a wonderful addition to a happy home. Dogues

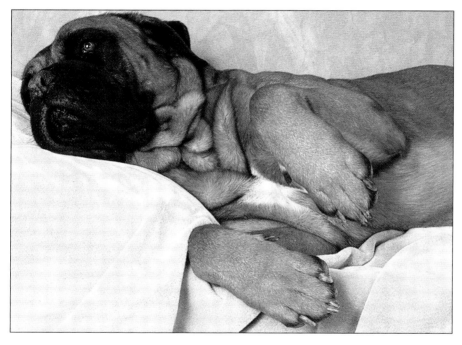

The Dogue will have no trouble making himself at home. If you choose to allow your Dogue on the couch, make sure he leaves some room for you!

Many believe that the Dogue de Bordeaux's intelligence and independent personality make it unresponsive to repeated instructions. Do not be discouraged. Every year many Dogues de Bordeaux successfully pass obedience exams and compete strongly in obedience trials. Practise patience, use rewards and be mentally stronger than your dog and you will prevail.

get along with other family pets, and if introduced early, can make friends with cats, birds and other dogs—depending on the compatibility of the collective personalities. There could be problems with having two male dogs with dominant personalities, and it is generally recommended to have dogs of opposite sex sharing a home. If you must have two males in the home, try to keep the age

29

A bitch with two of her offspring. Even young puppies have serious, intelligent looks on their faces.

difference as large as possible. Few young puppies will try to challenge the authority of a full-grown male and they will be quick to learn under the old dog's guidance and stature.

All of this is also valid for bitches. In both cases it is advisable to show the puppy to the 'old' dog and observe its reactions. Do not force the puppy's integration if the old dog

ACTIVITY
During playtime, training or exercise, you should be aware of your puppy's condition. Puppies should be given rest when needed. This should not be difficult to ascertain since puppies are usually very anxious, inquisitive and full of energy. When the puppy seems tired, he definitely needs to relax. The growth of the puppy is so fast that the tendons and ligaments—as for all large breeds—have to take a great strain. When taking the puppy for a walk, pace yourself. Increase the time/distance slowly during the first few months. A longer walk is possible after eight or nine months, but keep attuned to your puppy's condition. Remember that most of the growing process takes place during the first year. It shouldn't be a problem for a healthy Dogue de Bordeaux to go for a 10–20 kms walk, but not on a hot summer day.

The Dogue de Bordeaux loves to play and is always ready for fun, even in old age. Retrieving a stick or running after a ball may remind most Dogues de Bordeaux too much of work, but the same dog will be tireless while conquering an old towel or a potato sack.

Can a Dogue de Bordeaux run next to a bike? Yes and no. As long as you are not training for the Tour de France, it shouldn't

Unlike many other giant mastiffs, the Dogue de Bordeaux is an active, athletic animal that revels in a game of fetch with his master.

shows a defensive or aggressive reaction. If the old dog does not accept the puppy, it might be best to reconsider the acquisition, otherwise you will live in a permanent state of conflict.

As with other pets, the Dogue de Bordeaux will get along with children if introduced early and properly. Generally, there will be no problem if the child was there before the puppy. Always make sure that the child isn't abusive to the dog; it can be quite tempting for a young toddler to tease a tolerant Dogue de Bordeaux. This may be hard to believe, but adult supervision is more necessary for the Dogue's safety than the child's. By nature the Dogue is docile and merciful and loves human affection. Any Dogue de Bordeaux that is aggressive to humans without being instigated is atypical of the breed.

be a problem for your full-grown Dogue. A calm, even paced cycling around the park will be good and fun exercise for the both of you. As with walking, be sure to start off slowly and work your Dogue up to a pace you both can handle.

HEALTH CONCERNS

The Dogue lives on an average of eight to ten years. Like most large-boned dogs, hip dysplasia is the most common problem of the breed. Good breeders have their Dogues de Bordeaux screened for hip dysplasia. Unfortunately, the popularity of the breed has result-ed in many incompetent breeders who have bred unsound, inferior

You had better train your Dogue to HEEL or he will be dragging you on the other end of the lead.

Dogues with bad hips. Eliminating this condition is a constant battle.

In France at one time, the Dogue de Bordeaux was tested for hip dysplasia in the following manner, according to rare dog expert Carl Semencic:

'At two years of age, any Dogue that displays the physical and temperamental characteristics required for possible use in a breeding program is made to jump a fence that stands three feet high. Any Dogue that cannot easily clear the fence is excluded from any breeding plans.'

This may sound like a rather unscientific method of testing your Dogue, but it makes perfect sense. The Dogue de Bordeaux is supposed to be an athletically fit dog with powerful, muscular legs. Any Dogue that does not fit this description should not be consid-ered for breeding.

Heart murmurs and skin diseases are also problems with the Dogue. Heart murmurs can be attributed to the small gene pool that composes our Dogues today. Demodex mange is a skin problem rarely discussed amongst breeders, yet seems to be a problem for the Dogue de Bordeaux. This irritation is the result of a mite that lives on the dog and compromises the dog when the immune system is low. These mites feed faster than the body can reproduce cells, and they take over. Often this is mistaken for staff infection unless skin scrapings are done.

The Dogue de Bordeaux is a fast-growing dog. Puppies can gain 1–2 kgs a week on average and may experience Eosinphilic panosteitis (pano), better known as 'growing pains' or wandering lameness. Pano is an acute lameness unrelated to trauma. It shifts from one location to another and is accompanied by a fever.

Dogues de Bordeaux are also prone to bloat, a twisting of the stomach that could lead to death. Although the experts are not in agreement as to the exact causes, excessive exercise and excitement after eating and drinking can cause bloat. Bloat is most commonly traced to the dog's gulping of air that gets caught in its stomach. To prevent this, avoid feeding your Dogue de Bordeaux immediately before or after exercise, and feed several small portions throughout the day. Do not fill a huge dish with food and leave it there all day. Rather, keep feeding times consistent, and remove the food bowl from the dog's reach when he has finished eating. Leave water available during the day but not at feeding time. Many breeders recommend the use of a

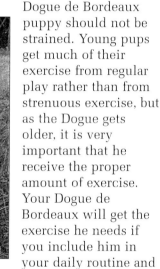

bowl stand to avoid the Dogue's craning its neck to reach its food bowls.

The Dogue needs a lot of exercise to develop its muscle structure. As with all large and heavy breeds, problems with tendons and ligaments can occur during the periods of quick growth. During these times the Dogue de Bordeaux puppy should not be strained. Young pups get much of their exercise from regular play rather than from strenuous exercise, but as the Dogue gets older, it is very important that he receive the proper amount of exercise. Your Dogue de Bordeaux will get the exercise he needs if you include him in your daily routine and take him on special jaunts such as hikes, hunts, jogs, etc. You should walk your Dogue at least twice a day and try to find time for an extended run or playtime a few times a week.

Special note: The Dogue de Bordeaux is very sensitive to anaesthesia. A 'normal' dose can be lethal. Take extra special care in choosing a veterinarian who is familiar with the breed and its idiosyncrasies—it could save your Dogue de Bordeaux's life!

Do not offer your Dogue small toys or anything that can be swallowed easily. Only offer large chew toys made especially for large dogs.

Dogue de Bordeaux

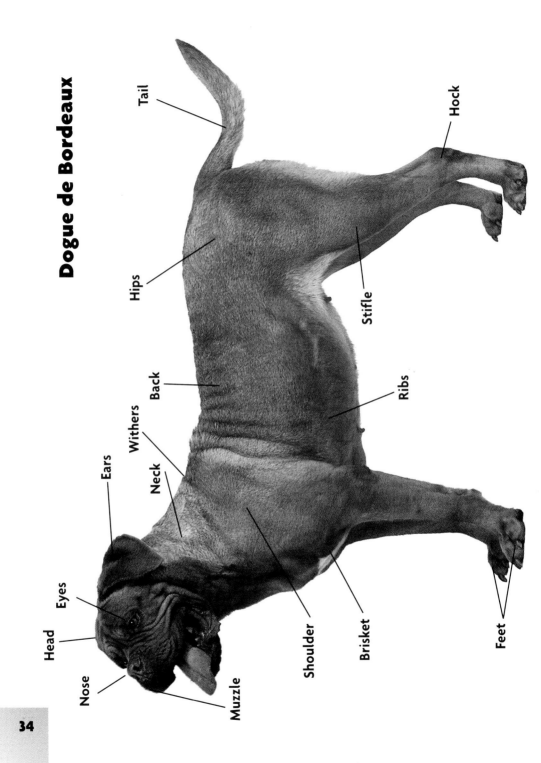

Tail

Hock

Hips

Stifle

Back

Ribs

Withers

Ears

Neck

Eyes

Head

Nose

Shoulder

Brisket

Feet

Muzzle

Dogue de Bordeaux

The standard, by which breeders breed and judges judge, is a written description of the perfect Dogue de Bordeaux. The current FCI standard, a few generations from the standard drafted by J Kunstler, was devised by Raymond Triquet, breeder and judge of the Dogue de Bordeaux, recognised as the world authority. This 'blueprint' of the perfect Dogue de Bordeaux is intended to assist the reader to envision what the ideal specimen of this breed should look like. Whilst standards are subjected to the reader's interpretation, this word picture is the accepted means by which show people evaluate their dogs. If a dog does not match closely to the standard, it will neither be included in a breeding programme nor campaigned as a show dog. Only the very best Dogues de Bordeaux should be bred in order to produce top-quality puppies in the next generation.

Pet owners should keep in mind that, although they may never intend to enter a dog show (or even attend one), the standard will help to learn what is acceptable in a good specimen and what is not. Physically the Dogue de Bordeaux is one of the most imposing, impressive and arguably beautiful of all dogs. Why settle for an untypical, unimpressive specimen? An educated approach to dog ownership is the best approach.

FÉDÉRATION CYNOLOGIQUE INTERNATIONALE STANDARD FOR THE DOGUE DE BORDEAUX

Origin and Purpose: Originated from France. Used in ancient times as a fighting dog, and used today as a companion and guard dog.

General Appearance: The Bordeaux Mastiff is a massive, powerfully built dog, with a very muscular body that retains a harmonious general outline. In stature, somewhat low to the ground. Distance from sternum to ground is at most equal or inferior to the depth of the chest, seen in profile and measured behind the elbows. Has the appearance of an athlete, imposing and proud, demanding respect.

Temperament: Assumes guard with vigilance and great courage, but without aggressiveness. Very attached to the master and very affectionate with children.

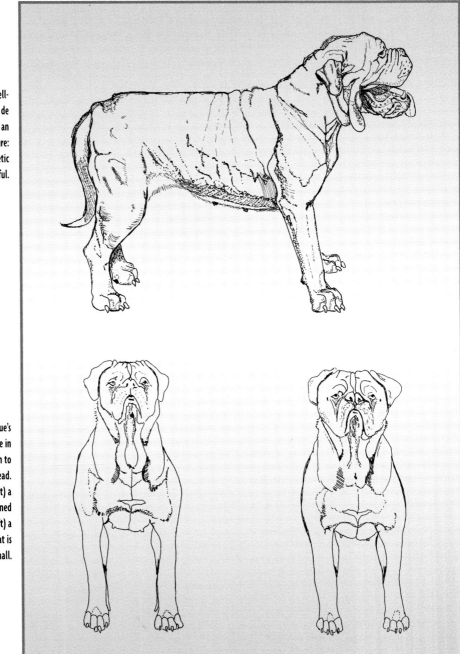

Side view of a well-built Dogue de Bordeaux. He is an imposing figure: muscular, athletic and powerful.

The size of a Dogue's body should be in direct relation to the size of its head. Examples of (right) a well-proportioned head and (left) a head that is too small.

Size: Weight for dogs is at least 50 kgs; for bitches, at least 45 kgs. Size should more or less correspond to head measurement. Males: 60–68 cms at the withers; bitches 58–66 cms at the withers.

Coat and Colour: *Colour:* Solid colour of mahogany (reddish brown), or in the range of the fawn shades. Good pigmentation is desirable. Small white patches on the chest and feet are allowed. *Coat:* Fine hair, short and soft to the touch.

Head: *Skull:* In the male, the perimeter of the skull measured at the level of its greatest width corresponds to the height at the withers. In the female, it may be slightly less. Its volume and its shape are the consequences of the very important development of the temporal, supraorbital ridges, zygomatic arches, and the spacing of the branches of the lower jaw. The upper region of the skull is slightly convex from side to side. Frontal–nasal depression of stop is very pronounced, almost at a right angle with the muzzle. The frontal groove is deep, diminishing toward the back of the head. The forehead dominates the face, yet is still wider than high.

Muzzle: Powerful, broad, thick, rather short, upper line very slightly concave, moderately obvious folds. Its width hardly decreases toward the end of the muzzle. When seen from above, it has the shape of a square. In relation to the upper region of the skull, the line of the muzzle forms an obtuse angle upwards. When head is held horizontally, the front end of the muzzle is blunt, thick and broad at the base, in front of a vertical tangent to the anterior face of the nose. Its perimeter is close to two-thirds of that of the head. Its length varies between a quarter and a third of the total length of the head, from the nose to the occipital crest.

Nose: Broad, well-opened nostrils, well pigmented black or brown according to the mask. Turned-up nose permitted.

Mouth: Jaws are very powerful and broad. Undershot bite. Lower jaw must project 0.5 cms minimum to 2 cms maximum. The incisors and canines must not be visible when mouth is closed. Teeth are very strong; strong canines; lower canines set wide apart and slightly curved. Incisors well aligned especially in lower jaw where they form an apparently straight line. Lips are thick, moderately pendulous, retractable, rounded over the lower jaw.

Eyes: Oval and set well apart. The space between the two inner angles of the eyelids equals about twice the length of the eye (eye opening). Frank expression. Hazel

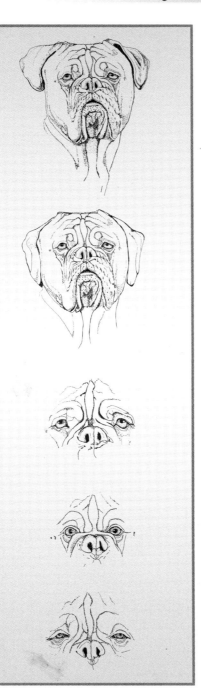

The ears should be relatively high set and short, not falling too far below the eye.

Ears are set too low on the head and are too long, reaching well below the nose.

The preferred facial features: eyes set well apart, oval, with frank expression.

Eyes are too round and set too close together. Face is too narrow overall.

Eyes are too slanted; face lacks the desired expression.

to dark brown for a dog with a black mask; lighter colour tolerated but not desirable in subjects with a red mask.

Ears: Relatively small, of a slightly darker colour than the coat. At its set on, the ear base is slightly raised in front but must fall back, without limpness along the cheeks. The tip is slightly rounded and must not reach much beyond the eye. Quite high set, at level of the upper line of the skull, the width of which they seem to accentuate even more.

Neck: Very strong, muscular, almost cylindrical. Enormous neck with ample skin, loose and supple. Average circumference equals almost that of the head. It is separated from the head by a slight transversal furrow, slightly curved. Its upper profile is slightly convex. The dewlap, well defined, starts at the level of the throat and forms folds down to the chest.

Forequarters: Strong bone structure, legs very muscular. Elbows neither turned in nor out too much. Forearm is straight or slightly inclined inward in order to get closer to the medium plane, especially with very broad chests. Pasterns are powerful, slightly sloping, sometimes a little turned. Feet are strong and tight. Nails curved and strong, preferably well pigmented. Pads well developed and supple.

A handsome Dogue de Bordeaux from America, owned by Andrea Switzer. Photograph by Close Encounters of the Furry Kind, Bane and Jeannie Harrison.

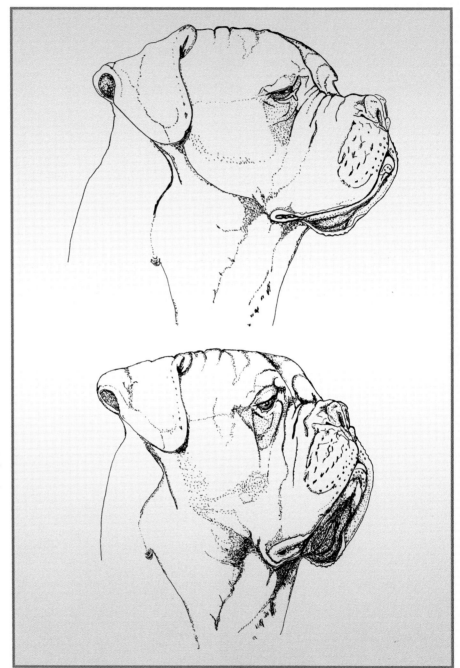

Head is longer rather than square, stop is not indented enough, muzzle is too long in relation to head.

Correct head: square, pronounced indentation of stop, relatively short muzzle.

40

Body: Chest is powerful, well ribbed up, broad, let down deeper than the elbows. Powerful forechest. Sternal ribs rounded. Other ribs well sprung and well let down. The circumference of the chest must be 0.25 m to 0.30 m superior to the height at the withers. Shoulders are powerful, muscles prominent, obliqueness of the shoulder blade about 45 degrees to the horizontal. Angle of the scapular-humeral articulation a little more than 90 degrees. Topline is straight, with a broad, muscular back. Withers well defined. Loin broad, rather short and solid. Rump moderately oblique down to the root of the tail. Underline is curved, from the long brisket to the tucked–up and firm abdomen.

Hindquarters: Thighs are well developed and thick, muscles visible. Stifle in a parallel plane to the vertical median plane or slightly turned inward or outward. Lower thigh is relatively short, muscular and well let down. Hock is short, sinewy, angle of the hock moderately open. When seen from behind, the parallel hind legs give the impression of power, although the hindquarters are slightly less broad than the forequarters.

Females: Identical characteristics, but less pronounced. Height is generally less than that of the males.

Gait: None given.

Tail: Very thick at the base. The tip does not reach below the hock. Carried low, deeply set. Hanging when at rest, generally raised from 90–121 degrees in relation to this vertical position when dog is active.

Faults: Small head, not in proportion to the height at the withers, too long, narrow piped, round, oval, flat forehead. Absence of medial groove. Occipital protuberance too obvious. Naso–frontal angle too acute or too blunt. Wrinkles too close together, not mobile. Muzzle that is too long, too short, narrow, shallow, pointed, snipy (nose in front of lips). Muzzle parallel with the upper line of the skull, down faced, fleshy below the eyes. Nose too narrow, tight nostrils, butterfly nose, dudley nose (flesh coloured). Jaws of equal length (pinscher bite), scissors bite, overshot, exaggerated or insufficient, undershot mouth. Teeth that are weak or badly lined up. Lips that are excessively long and floppy (non retractable), too short. Underdeveloped cheeks, flabby, lean or gaunt. Eyes that are small, round, too sunken, protruding, close together, too light, staring expression, showing haw. Ears too flabby, too short, too long, cropped, inset or carriage too high, pricked, rose ears, laterally

The female Dogue, shown here, is slightly smaller than the male.

(FACING PAGE) Head study of a typical male Dogue.

set far apart, too low set. Slender, thin, long, or flat neck. Skin too tight or an exaggerated hanging dewlap. Narrow chest, not very long. Ribs too flat, or, on the contrary, barrel shaped. Brisket concave when seen from the front. Insufficiently muscled shoulders, or being too straight. Saddle back, humped back, weak loin, overbuilt rump, rump rounded or steeped. Tail that is carried sideways, truncated, broken twisted, docked, caudal vertebrate fused (knotted tail). Tail carried vertically or rolled up. Tufted tip. Absence of tail, even accidental, is always suspect. Pendulous abdomen, or too tucked up. Forequarters of light bone, insufficient muscle. In or out too much at the elbows. Forearm too bowed. Pastern turned in or out too much, down in the pasterns. Flat, hare feet or splayed toes. Flat or thin hindquarters. Stifle too much turned out or in. Hock that is over angulated or too straight, dewclaws.

Disqualifications: Wall eyed or flesh coloured spots on the eyelids.

Note: Male dogs should have two apparently normal testicles fully descended into the scrotum.

43

Dogue de Bordeaux

OWNER CONSIDERATIONS

How remarkable, unusual and alluring is the Dogue de Bordeaux! Who could deny the attention a pet owner would attract strolling along the thoroughfare with a full-grown Dogue de Bordeaux? Not to mention the attention an irresistible Dogue puppy receives!

Who can resist a puppy...especially breed as fascinating as the Dogue de Bordeaux?

Whether you are seeking a puppy simply as a house companion and family pet, a show dog, a hunting dog, or a competition dog, there are many serious factors governing your choice. You believe that you have enough time to devote to your new Dogue de Bordeaux. Even a pet Dogue de Bordeaux will require considerable time to train. Naturally, a guard or obedience/agility dog will require hours of special training. Do not take the acquisition of a Dogue de Bordeaux lightly—everything about the Dogue is heavy! This is a demanding dog who will want to make you his number-one priority: Are you prepared for that commitment that is accompanied by this giant's steadfast devotion, a bucket of drool, unabashed affection and a virtual tonne of 'poop.'

Consider the exercise that a dog as active as the Dogue de Bordeaux will require. You have a fenced garden, so there is no worry that your curious pup will not go wandering down the lane to find your neighbours and their dogs and cats and horses! If you are not committed to the welfare and whole existence of this powerful, purposeful animal; if, in the simplest, most basic example, you are not willing to walk your dog daily, despite the weather, do not choose a Dogue de Bordeaux as a companion.

Space is another huge consideration. The Dogue de Bordeaux in early puppyhood may be well accommodated in a corner of your kitchen, but after only six months, when the puppy is likely over 90 pounds, larger space certainly will be required. No matter how affectionate your Dogue puppy is in your company, he cannot exist in a two-room flat. You will have to train your Dogue de Bordeaux to understand the house rules, so that you can trust him in every room of your house. Of course, puppy-proofing for such a powerful animal is vital. The Dogue de Bordeaux can likely eat anything it wants—from his morning victuals to your slippers to your bedroom furniture!

There are the usual problems associated with puppies of any breed like the damages likely to be sustained by your floors, furniture, flowers and, not least of all, to your freedom (of movement), as in holiday or weekend trips. With the Dogue de Bordeaux, these demands and potential hazards are multiplied tenfold. This union is a serious affair and should be deeply considered but once decided, your choice of a Dogue de Bordeaux can be the most rewarding of all.

A few suggestions will help in the purchase of your dog.

ACQUIRING A PUPPY
The recommended method of obtaining a purebred puppy of any breed is to seek out a reputable breeder. Given the relative rareness of the Dogue de Bordeaux, you will not have to

> **DID YOU KNOW?**
> Unfortunately, when a puppy is bought by someone who does not take into consideration the time and attention that dog ownership requires, it is the puppy who suffers when he is either abandoned or placed in a shelter by a frustrated owner. So all of the 'homework' you do in preparation for your pup's arrival will benefit you both. The more informed you are, the more you will know what to expect and the better equipped you will be to handle the ups and downs of raising a puppy. Hopefully, everyone in the household is willing to do his part in raising and caring for the pup. The anticipation of owning a dog often brings a lot of promises from excited family members: 'I will walk him every day,' 'I will feed him,' 'I will housebreak him,' etc., but these things take time and effort, and promises can easily be forgotten once the novelty of the new pet has worn off.

worry so much about recognising and avoiding novice breeders. Such novice breeders advertise at 'attractive prices' in the local newspapers. Generally these inexperienced people are probably kind enough toward their dogs, but do not have the expertise or facilities required to successfully raise a litter of Dogue puppies. A lack of proper feeding can cause indigestion, rickets, weak bones, poor teeth and other problems. Veterinary bills may soon distort initial savings into financial, or worse, emotional loss. More often than not, these breeders sell puppies at the same price as a professional breeder, so there is never a savings.

The Dogue de Bordeaux, a fairly recent import into the

DID YOU KNOW?
You should not even think about buying a puppy that looks sick, undernourished, overly frightened or nervous. Sometimes a timid puppy will warm up to you after a 30-minute 'let's-get-acquainted' session.

United Kingdom, has yet to attract a large number of breeders, so the breeders who exist are both reliable and fair. The best dogs of course are bred on the Continent, in France, the breed's homeland, as well as Holland and Germany. Many British breeders specialise in lines from these countries, so it is quite possible to acquire a well-bred Dogue de Bordeaux from these breeders.

When you visit the breeder, you will have ample opportunity to evaluate the puppies, the dam and the facility. Whenever possible, the breeder will present the dam, and hopefully the sire, to you. Viewing the parents of your chosen litter speaks volumes about the expected future quality, temperament, size, etc., of the pups. Actually meeting the dam is better than any promise the breeder could make regarding the excellence of the litter. Always keep in mind that the dam may appear somewhat bedraggled and 'overworked.' Caring for a large litter of Bordeaux pups for six to eight weeks could drain the life

DID YOU KNOW?
Your selection of a good puppy can be determined by your needs. A show potential or a good pet? It is your choice. Every puppy, however, should be of good temperament. Although show-quality puppies are bred and raised with emphasis on physical conformation, responsible breeders strive for equally good temperament. Do not buy from a breeder who concentrates solely on physical beauty at the expense of personality.

out of any bitch! Don't expect her to resemble the lovely photographs in this book in a show pose. She has been working hard for months.

When evaluating the litter, note the way the puppies move. The Dogue de Bordeaux, even in puppyhood, should show a fair amount of coordination. Despite the breed's giant stature, the Dogue is an athletic and agile animal. Don't expect the pup to be light on his big feet, but there should be no tendency to stumble or drag the hind feet. Look at the mouth to make sure that the bite is undershot, meaning that the lower jaw protrudes further than the upper jaw, as in a Bulldog, though not as exaggerated. If you have any doubts, ask to see the parents' mouths.

Consider the temperament of the litter. The pups should be friendly and outgoing, interested in their surroundings and amenable to handling. With a dog

Selecting from a litter of Dogues is not an easy task. Not only do you want the one whose personality best suits you, but you want one who is healthy and sound.

as large as the Dogue, temperament is of paramount importance. Whilst you want a Dogue de Bordeaux that is handsome, impressive and totally representative of its breed, you also want a Dogue that is friendly, trustworthy and 100-percent reliable around children. Given the power of this dog, you cannot afford to sacrifice the temperament of your chosen puppy. If the puppy has been properly socialised (that is, introduced to people, other dogs, situations outside his whelping pen), he should be personable and alert. Avoid a shy, overly aggressive or 'spooky' puppy. If this describes the whole litter, it's time

DID YOU KNOW?

Your puppy should have a well-fed appearance but not a distended abdomen, which may indicate worms or incorrect feeding, or both. The body should be firm, with a solid feel. The skin of the abdomen should be pale pink and clean, without signs of scratching or rash. Check the hind legs to make certain that dewclaws were removed, if any were present at birth.

47

to visit a new breeder. Bordeaux pups are absolutely delicious, irresistible and disarmingly adorable—don't be seduced by a litter that is not stable and friendly. That is your most important consideration.

COMMITMENT OF OWNERSHIP
After considering all of these factors, you have most likely already made some very

important decisions about selecting your puppy. You have chosen a Dogue, which means that you have decided which characteristics you want in a dog and what type of dog will best fit into your family and lifestyle. If you have selected a breeder, you have gone a step further—you have done your research and found a responsible, conscientious person who breeds quality Dogues and who should be a reliable source of help as you and your puppy adjust to life together. If you have observed a litter in action, you have gotten a firsthand look at the dynamics of a puppy 'pack' and, you have learned about each pup's individual personality—perhaps you have even found one that particularly appeals to you.

However, even if you have not yet found the Dogue puppy of your dreams, observing pups will help you learn to recognise certain behaviour and to determine what a pup's behaviour indicates about his temperament. You will be able to pick out which pups are the leaders, which ones are less outgoing, which ones are confident and which ones are shy, playful, friendly, aggressive, etc. Equally important, you will learn to recognise how a healthy pup should look and act. All of these things will help you in your search, and when you find the Dogue that was meant for you, you will know it!

DID YOU KNOW?

Two important documents you will get from the breeder are the pup's pedigree and registration papers. The breeder should register the litter and each pup with The Kennel Club, and it is necessary for you to have the paperwork if you plan on showing or breeding in the future.

Make sure you know the breeder's intentions on which type of registration he will obtain for the pup. There are limited registrations which may prohibit the dog from being shown or from competing in non-conformation trials such as Working or Agility if the breeder feels that the pup is not of sufficient quality to do so. There is also a type of registration that will permit the dog in non-conformation competition only.

If your dog is registered with a Kennel-Club-recognised breed club, then you can register the pup with The Kennel Club yourself. Your breeder can assist you with the specifics of the registration process.

Dogues de Bordeaux grow quickly and will become very large animals. They take up a lot of space, their appetites are huge and they need exercise every day. Are you up to this responsibility?

Researching your breed, selecting a responsible breeder and observing as many pups as possible are all important steps on the way to dog ownership. It may seem like a lot of effort...and you have not even brought the pup home yet! Remember, you cannot be too careful when deciding on the type of dog you want and finding out about your prospective pup's background. Buying a puppy is not—or should not be— just another whimsical purchase. In fact, this is one instance in which you actually do get to choose your own family! But, you may be thinking, buying a puppy should be fun—it should not be so serious and so much work. If you

keep in mind that your puppy is not a cuddly stuffed toy or decorative lawn ornament, but a real member of your family, you will

DID YOU KNOW?
Breeders rarely release puppies until they are eight to ten weeks of age. This is an acceptable age for most breeds of dog, excepting toy breeds which are not released until around 12 weeks, given their petite sizes. If a breeder has a puppy that is 12 weeks or more, it is likely well socialised and housetrained. Be sure that it is otherwise healthy before deciding to take it home.

Buying a Dogue puppy should be a well-thought-out decision and not a whimsy...be careful! If you have the ability to see a Dogue puppy with at least one of the parents, you will have a good idea of the pup's personality.

DID YOU KNOW?

If you lead an erratic, unpredictable life, with daily or weekly changes in your work requirements, consider the problems of owning a puppy. The new puppy has to be fed regularly, socialised (loved, petted, handled, introduced to other people) and, most importantly, allowed to visit outdoors for toilet training. As the dog gets older, it can be more tolerant of deviations in its feeding and toilet relief.

realise that while buying a puppy is a pleasurable and exciting endeavour, it is not something to be taken lightly. Relax...the fun will start when the pup comes home!

Always keep in mind that a puppy is nothing more than a baby in a furry disguise...a baby who is virtually helpless in a human world and who trusts his owner for fulfilment of his basic needs for survival. That goes beyond food, water and shelter; your pup needs care, protection, guidance and love. If you are not prepared to commit to this, then you are not prepared to own a dog.

Wait a minute, you say. How hard could this be? All of my neighbours own dogs and they seem to be doing just fine. Why should I have to worry about all of this? Well, you should not worry about it; in fact, you will probably find that once your Dogue pup gets used to his new home, he will fall into his place in the family quite naturally. But it never hurts to emphasise the commitment of dog ownership. With some time and patience, it is really not too difficult to raise a curious and exuberant Dogue pup to be a well-adjusted and well-mannered adult dog—a dog that could be your most loyal friend.

PREPARING PUPPY'S PLACE IN YOUR HOME

Researching your breed and finding a breeder are only two aspects of the 'homework' you will have to do before bringing your Dogue puppy home. You will also have to prepare your home and family for the new addition. Much as you would prepare a nursery for a newborn baby, you will need to designate a place in your home that will be the puppy's own. How you prepare your home will depend on how much freedom the dog will be allowed. Will he spend most of his time in the house or

Your new puppy will have to be taught where he is allowed and where is off limits. Training is key to convincing your Dogue where he belongs.

will he be primarily an outdoor dog? Whatever you decide, you must ensure that he has a place that he can 'call his own.'

When you bring your new puppy into your home, you are bringing him into what will become his home as well. Obviously, you did not buy a

> **DID YOU KNOW?**
> If the breeder from whom you are buying a puppy asks you a lot of personal questions, do not be insulted. Such a breeder wants to be sure that you will be a fit provider for his puppy.

puppy so that he could take over your house, but in order for a puppy to grow into a stable, well-adjusted dog; he has to feel comfortable in his surroundings. Remember, he is leaving the warmth and security of his mother and littermates, plus the familiarity of the only place he has ever known, so it is important to make his transition as easy as possible. By preparing a place in your home for the puppy, you are making him feel as welcome as possible in a strange new place. It should not take him long to get used to it, but the sudden shock of being transplanted is somewhat traumatic for a young pup. Imagine how a small child would

feel in the same situation—that is how your puppy must be feeling. It is up to you to reassure him and to let him know, 'Little fellow, you are going to like it here!'

WHAT YOU SHOULD BUY
CRATE

To someone unfamiliar with the use of crates in dog training, it may seem like punishment to shut a dog in a crate. This is not the case at all. Although all breeders do not advocate crate training, more and more breeders and trainers are recommending crates as a preferred tool for pet puppies as well as show puppies. Crates are not cruel—crates have many humane and highly effective uses in dog care and training. For example, crate training is a much recommended and successful housebreaking method; a crate can keep your dog safe during travel; and, perhaps most importantly, a crate provides your dog with a place of his own in your home. It serves

> **DID YOU KNOW?**
> The cost of food must also be mentioned. All dogs need a good quality food with an adequate supply of protein to develop their bones and muscles properly. Most dogs are not picky eaters but unless fed properly they can quickly succumb to skin problems.

as a 'doggie bedroom' of sorts—your Dogue can curl up in his crate when he wants to sleep or when he just needs a rest. Many dogs sleep in their crates overnight. When lined with soft blankets and filled with his favourite toys and stuffed pals, a crate becomes a cosy pseudo-den for your dog. Like his ancestors, he too will seek out the comfort and retreat of a den—you just happen to be providing him with something a little more luxurious than leaves and twigs lining a dirty ditch.

As far as purchasing a crate, the type that you buy is up to you. It will most likely be one of the two most popular types: wire or fibreglass. The wire crate is more open, allowing the air to flow through and affording the dog a view of what is going on around him. A fibreglass crate, is sturdier and is preferable as a travel crate since it provides more protection for the dog. The size of the crate is another thing to consider. Puppies do not stay puppies

forever—in fact, sometimes it seems as if they grow right before your eyes. A medium-sized crate may be fine for a very young Dogue pup, but it will not do him much good for long! Unless you

PHOTO COURTESY OF DOSKOCIL.

Your local pet shop should be the source for all of your pet supplies. Most pet shops have a large variety of crates in all sizes, weights and prices. You need the largest size for your Dogue puppy because they grow so large.

Wicker dog beds are satisfactory for very young puppies, but when they start to chew, the wicker will be the first to go!

The puppy's bedding is important. Take the advice of the breeder as to which bedding you should use to make your puppy comfortable.

DID YOU KNOW?

During crate training, you should partition off the section of the crate in which the pup stays. If he is given too big an area, this will hinder your training efforts. Crate training is based on the fact that a dog does not like to soil his sleeping quarters, so it is ineffective to keep a pup in a crate that is so big that he can eliminate in one end and get far enough away from it to sleep. Also, you want to make the crate den-like for the pup. Blankets and a favourite toy will make the crate cosy for the small pup; as he grows, you may want to evict some of his 'roommates' to make more room.

It will take some coaxing at first, but be patient. Given some time to get used to it, your pup will adapt to his new home-within-a-home quite nicely.

have the money and the inclination to buy a new crate every time your pup has a growth spurt, it is better to get one that will accommodate your dog both as a pup and at full size. The largest crate available will be necessary for a full-grown Dogue de Bordeaux.

BEDDING

Veterinary bedding in the dog's crate will help the dog feel more at home and you may also like to pop in a blanket. This will take

the place of the leaves, twigs, etc., that the pup would use in the wild to make a den and the pup can make his own 'burrow' in the crate. Although your pup is far removed from his den-making ancestors, the denning instinct is still a part of his genetic makeup. Until you bring your pup home, he has been sleeping amidst the warmth of his mother and littermates, and while a blanket is not the same as a warm, breathing body, it still provides heat and something with which to snuggle. You will want to wash your pup's bedding frequently in case he has an accident in his crate, and replace or remove any blanket that becomes ragged and starts to fall apart.

A brightly coloured toy looks enticing to a Dogue puppy, but the small knobs can be chewed off and swallowed easily. This could cause choking or a life-threatening intestinal blockage.

Toys

Toys are a must for dogs of all ages, especially for curious playful pups. Puppies are the 'children' of the dog world, and what child does not love toys? Chew toys provide enjoyment to

DID YOU KNOW?

With a big variety of dog toys available, and so many that look like they would be a lot of fun for a dog, be careful in your selection. It is amazing what a set of puppy teeth can do to an innocent-looking toy, so, obviously, safety is a major consideration. Be sure to choose the most durable products that you can find. Hard nylon bones and toys are a safe bet, and many of them are offered in different scents and flavours that will be sure to capture your dog's attention. It is always fun to play a game of catch with your dog, and there are balls and flying discs that are specially made to withstand dog teeth.

Do not use flimsy toys or toys made for children. Only buy toys sold in pet shops that are solely intended for dogs' use.

55

One of the best chew devices is heavy nylon rope that has been boiled in to anneal the threads and flavoured to make it attractive to dogs. It is not only entertaining but it also reduces the plaque on the Dogue's teeth.

both dog and owner—your dog will enjoy playing with his favourite toys, whilst you will enjoy the fact that they distract him from your expensive shoes and leather sofa. Puppies love to chew. In fact, chewing is a physical need for pups when they are teething, and everything looks appetising! The full range of your possessions—from old dishcloth to Oriental rug—are fair game in the eyes of a teething pup. Puppies are not discerning when it comes to finding something to literally 'sink their teeth into'— everything tastes great!

Pet shops carry many special toys made for dogs. Do not use toys made for humans.

Stuffed toys are another option; these are good to put in the dog's crate to give him some company, but be careful of these, as a pup can de-stuff one pretty quickly. Stay away from stuffed toys with small plastic eyes or other parts that could choke a pup. Similarly, squeaky toys are quite popular. There are dogs that will come running from anywhere in the house at the first sound from their favourite squeaky friend, but if a pup de-stuffs one of these, the small plastic squeaker inside can be dangerous if swallowed. Monitor the condition of your pup's toys carefully and get rid of any that have been chewed to the point of becoming potentially dangerous.

Be careful of natural bones, which have a tendency to splinter into sharp, dangerous pieces. Also be careful of rawhide, which can turn into pieces that are easy to swallow or a mushy mess on your carpet.

You should be prepared with a suitable crate, toys, water and food bowls and a few other essentials BEFORE you bring home the Dogue.

LEAD

A nylon lead is probably the best option as it is the most resistant to puppy teeth should your pup take a liking to chewing on his lead. This habit should be nipped in the bud, but if your pup likes to chew on his lead, he has a very slim chance of being able to chew through strong nylon. Nylon leads are also lightweight, which is good for a young Dogue who is just getting used to the idea of walking on a lead. For everyday walking and safety purposes, the nylon lead is a good choice. As your pup grows up and gets used to walking on the lead, and can do it politely, you may want to purchase a flexible lead, which allows you to extend the length to

While thin nylon leads are suitable for very young Dogue puppies and for the show ring, they are not strong enough for regular walks and exercise.

57

Your local pet shop should have a complete stock of leads and leashes from which you can select the one most suitable for the size of your Dogue.

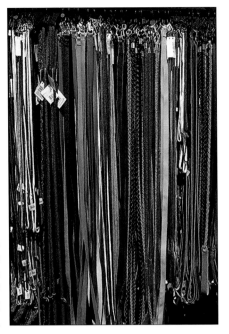

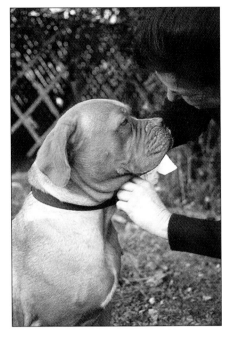

The collar for a growing Dogue should not just be larger, but made of stronger material as well.

When buying a collar for your Dogue puppy, keep in mind that the puppy will grow quickly and the collar must increase in size to keep pace with this growth.

give the dog a broader area to explore or to pull in the lead when you want to keep him close. There are special leads for training purposes, and specially made leather harnesses for the working Dogue, but these are not necessary for routine walks. As your Dogue matures, you will want to purchase something stronger, like a thicker leather lead.

COLLAR

Your pup should get used to wearing a collar at all times since you will want to attach his ID tags to his collar and you have to attach the lead to something! Make sure that the collar fits

snugly enough so that the pup cannot wriggle out of it, but is loose enough so that it will not be uncomfortably tight around the pup's neck. You should be able to fit a finger between the pup and

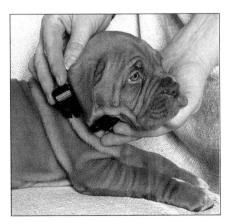

CHOOSE THE PROPER COLLAR

The BUCKLE COLLAR is the standard collar used for everyday purpose. Be sure that you adjust the buckle on growing puppies. Check it every day. It can become too tight overnight! These collars can be made of leather or nylon. Attach your dog's identification tags to this collar.

Buckle Collar

The CHOKE CHAIN is the usual collar recommended for training. It is constructed of highly polished steel so that it slides easily through the stainless steel loop. The idea is that the dog controls the pressure around its neck and he will stop pulling if the collar becomes uncomfortable. Never leave a choke collar on your dog when not training.

Choke Chain

The HALTER is for a trained dog that has to be restrained to prevent running away, chasing a cat and the like. Considered the most humane of all collars, it is frequently used on smaller dogs for which collars are not comfortable.

Halter

Your local pet shop should carry a variety of dog bowls and dishes. Sturdy plastic bowls are very popular, as well as more chew-resistant stainless steel and heavy crockery bowls.

the collar. It may take some time for your pup to get used to wearing the collar, but soon he will not even notice that it is there. Choke collars are made for training, but should only be used by an owner who knows exactly how to use it. If you use a stronger leather lead or a chain lead to walk your Dogue, you will need a stronger collar.

FOOD AND WATER BOWLS

Your pup will need two bowls, one for food and one for water. You may want two sets of bowls, one for inside and one for outside, depending on where the dog will be fed and where he will be spending most of his time. Stainless steel or sturdy plastic bowls are popular choices. Plastic bowls are more chewable, and dogs tend not to chew on the steel variety, which can be sanitised. Some dog owners like to put their dogs' food and water bowls on a specially made elevated stand. This brings the food closer to the dog's level so he does not have to bend down as far, aiding his

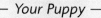

digestion and helping to guard against bloat or gastric torsion in deep-chested dogs. It is important to buy sturdy bowls since everything is in danger of being chewed by puppy teeth and you do not want your dog to be constantly chewing apart his bowl (for his safety and for your wallet!).

CLEANING SUPPLIES

Plan on doing a lot of cleaning until your pup is housetrained. Accidents will occur, which is okay for now because he does not know any better. All you can do is clean up any 'accidents'—old rags, towels, newspapers and a safe disinfectant are good to have on hand.

You can purchase a device from your local pet shop that will take the work out of cleaning up after your dog. Make it a habit to clean up when your dog relieves himself, regardless of where it occurs.

DID YOU KNOW?

Grooming tools, collars, leashes, dog beds and, of course, toys will be an expense to you when you first obtain your pup, and the cost will trickle on throughout your dog's lifetime. If your puppy damages or destroys your possessions (as most puppies surely will!) or something belonging to a neighbour, you can calculate additional expense. There is also flea and pest control, which every dog owner faces more than once. You must be able to handle the financial responsibility of owning a dog.

BEYOND THE BASICS

The items previously discussed are the bare necessities. You will discover what else you need as you go along—grooming supplies, flea/tick protection, baby gates to partition a room, etc.—these things will vary depending on your situation. In the beginning, it is only important that you have everything you need to feed and make your Dogue comfortable in his first few days at home.

PUPPY-PROOFING YOUR HOME

Aside from making sure that your Dogue will be comfortable in your home, you also have to make sure that your home is safe for your Dogue. This means taking precautions to make sure that your pup will not get into anything he should not get into and that there is nothing within his reach that

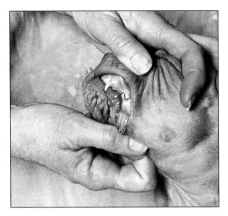

Examine your Dogue's teeth regularly. Dogues must chew to help their teeth grow in straight and strong and to keep them clean. It also exercises their strong jaw muscles.

may harm him should he sniff it, chew it, inspect it, etc. While you are primarily concerned with your pup's safety, you do not want your belongings to be ruined. Breakables should be placed out

of reach if your dog is to have full run of the house. If he is to be limited to certain places within the house, keep any potentially dangerous items in the 'off-limits' areas. Electrical cords should be fastened tightly against the wall. They can pose a danger should the puppy decide to taste them—and who is going to convince a pup that loose wires would not make great chew toys? If your dog is going to spend time in a crate, make sure that there is nothing near his crate that he can reach if he sticks his curious little nose or paws through the openings. Just as you would with a child, keep all household cleaners and chemicals where the pup cannot get to them.

It is just as important to make sure that the outside of your home is safe. Your puppy should never be unsupervised, but a pup let loose in the garden will want to run and explore, and he should be granted that freedom. Do not let a fence give you a false sense of security; you would be surprised how crafty (and persistent) a dog can be in figuring out how to dig under or climb over a fence. The remedy is to make the fence high enough so that it really is impossible for your dog to get over it

(about 3 metres should suffice), and well embedded into the ground. Be sure to repair or secure any gaps in the fence and check the fence periodically to ensure that it remains in good shape. A very determined pup may return to the same spot to 'work on it' until he is able to get through.

FIRST TRIP TO THE VET

You have picked out your puppy, your home and family are ready, now all you have to do is pick your Dogue up from the breeder and the fun begins, right? Well…not so fast. You need to prepare for your pup's first trip to the veterinary surgeon. Perhaps the breeder can recommend someone in the area that specialises in Dogues, or maybe you know some other Dogue owners who can suggest a good vet. Either

Plan a trip to the vet as one of the first things you do with your new Dogue de Bordeaux puppy.

Your puppy will need love, attention and gentle reassurance to make his transition into your home an easy one.

way, you should have an appointment arranged for your pup before you pick him up, and plan on taking him for a check-up before bringing him home.

The pup's first visit will consist of an overall examination to make sure that the pup does not have any problems that are not apparent to the eye. The veterinary surgeon will also set up a schedule for the pup's vaccinations. The breeder will inform you of which ones the pup has already received and the vet can continue from there.

INTRODUCTION TO THE FAMILY

Everyone in the house will be excited about the puppy coming home and will want to pet him and play with him, but it is best to make the introduction low-key so as not to overwhelm the puppy. He is already apprehensive. It is the first time he has been separated from his mother and the breeder, and the ride to your home is likely the first time he has been in an auto. The last thing you want to do is smother him, as this will only frighten him further. Human contact is extremely necessary at this stage, because this is the time when a connection between the pup and his human family are formed. Gentle petting

Your house is a big, unfamiliar place for a small Dogue puppy—especially on his first night. It will take him some time to get used to his new home.

and soothing words should help console him, as will putting him down and letting him explore on his own (under your watchful eye, of course).

The pup may approach the family members or may busy himself with exploring for awhile. Gradually, each person should spend some time with the pup, one at a time, crouching down to get as close to the pup's level as possible while letting him sniff their hands and petting him gently. He needs human attention and he needs to be touched in order to form an immediate bond. Just remember that the pup is experiencing a lot of things for the first time, at the same time. There are new people, new noises, new smells, and new things to investigate. So be gentle, be affectionate and be as comforting as you can.

YOUR PUP'S FIRST NIGHT HOME

You have travelled home with your new charge safely in his basket or crate. He's been to the vet for a thorough check-over. He's been weighed, his papers examined; perhaps he's even been vaccinated and wormed. He's met the family, licked the whole family, including the excited children and the less-than-happy cat. He's explored his area, his new bed, the garden and anywhere else he's been permitted. He's eaten his first meal at home and relieved himself in the proper place. He's heard lots of new sounds, smelled new friends and seen more of the outside world than ever before.

That was the just the first day!

Whether a dog bed or a crate, make the place where your puppy sleeps comfortable.

DID YOU KNOW?

An important consideration to be discussed is the sex of your puppy. For a family companion, a bitch may be the better choice, considering the female's inbred concern for all young creatures and her accompanying tolerance and patience. It is always advised to spay a pet bitch, which may guarantee her a longer life.

DID YOU KNOW?

Training your puppy takes much patience and can be frustrating at times, but you should see results from your efforts. If you have a puppy that seems untrainable, take him to a trainer or behaviourist. The dog may have a personality problem that requires the help of a professional, or perhaps you need help in learning how to train your dog.

He's worn out and is ready for bed…or so you think!

It's puppy's first night and you are ready to say 'Good night'— keep in mind that this is puppy's first night sleeping alone. His dam and littermates are no longer at paw's length and he's a bit scared, cold and lonely. Be reassuring to your new family member but this is not the time to spoil him and give in to his inevitable whining.

Puppies whine. They whine to let the others know where they are and to get company. Place your pup in his new bed or crate in his room and close the door. Mercifully, he may fall asleep without a peep. If the inevitable occurs, ignore the whining, he is fine. Be strong and keep his interest in mind. Do not become guilty and visit the pup. He will fall asleep.

Many breeders recommend placing a piece of bedding from

his former homestead in his new bed so that he recognises the scent of his littermates. Others still advise placing a hot water bottle in his bed for warmth. The latter may be a good idea provided the pup doesn't attempt to suckle—he'll get good and wet and may not fall asleep so fast.

Puppy's first night can be somewhat stressful for the pup and his new family. Remember that you are setting the tone of nighttime at your house. Unless you want to play with your pup every evening at 10 pm, midnight and 2 am, don't initiate the habit. Your family will thank you, and so will your pup!

PREVENTING PUPPY PROBLEMS
SOCIALISATION

Now that you have done all of the preparatory work and have helped your pup get accustomed to his new home and family, it is time for you to have some fun! Socialising your Dogue pup gives you the opportunity to show off your new friend. Your pup gets to reap the benefits of being an adorable furry creature that people will want to pet and, in general, think is absolutely precious!

Besides getting to know his new family, your puppy should be exposed to other people, animals and situations, but of course he must not come into close contact with dogs you don't know well

A well-socialized puppy will act less fearful and timid around unknown people and circumstances.

until his course of injections is fully complete. This will help him become well adjusted and less prone to being timid or fearful of the new things he will encounter. Your pup's socialisation began at the breeder's, but now it is your responsibility. The socialisation he receives up until the age of 12 weeks is the most critical, as this

DID YOU KNOW?
Thorough socialisation includes not only meeting new people but also being introduced to new experiences such as riding in the auto, having his coat brushed, hearing the television, walking in a crowd—the list is endless. The more your pup experiences, and the more positive the experiences are, the less of a shock and the less scary it will be for your pup to encounter new things.

is the time when he forms his impressions of the outside world. Be especially careful during the eight-to-ten-week period, known as the fear period. The interaction he receives during this time should be gentle and reassuring Lack of socialisation can manifest itself in fear and aggression as the dog grows up. He needs lots of human interaction, affection, handling and exposure to other animals.

Once your pup has received his necessary vaccinations, feel free to take him out and about (on his lead, of course). Take him around the neighbourhood, take him on your daily errands, let people pet him, let him meet other dogs and pets, etc. Puppies do not have to try to make friends. There will be no shortage of people who will want to introduce themselves. Just make sure that you carefully supervise each interaction. You want your dog to be comfortable around everyone. If the neighbourhood children want to say hello, that is great. Children and pups most often make great companions, but sometimes an excited child can unintentionally handle a pup too roughly, or an overzealous pup can playfully nip a little too hard. You want to make socialisation experiences positive ones. What a pup learns during this very formative stage will impact his attitude toward future

encounters. A pup that has a bad experience with a child may grow up to be a dog that is shy around or aggressive toward children.

CONSISTENCY IN TRAINING
Dogs, being pack animals, need a leader or they will try to establish dominance in their packs. When you bring a dog into your family, who becomes the leader and who becomes the 'pack' are entirely up to you! Your pup's intuitive quest for dominance, coupled with the fact that it is nearly impossible to look at an adorable Dogue pup, with his 'puppy-dog' eyes and not cave in, give the pup an unfair advantage in getting the upper hand! A pup will definitely test the waters to see what he can and cannot get away with. Do not give in to those pleading eyes—stand your ground when it comes to disciplining the pup and make sure that all family members do the same. Avoid discrepancies by having all members of the household decide on the rules before the pup even comes home...and be consistent in enforcing them! It will only confuse the pup if Mother tells him to get off the couch when he is used to sitting up there with Father to watch the nightly news. Early training shapes the dog's personality, so you cannot be unclear in what you expect.

COMMON PUPPY PROBLEMS

The best way to prevent problems is to be proactive in stopping an undesirable behaviour as soon as it starts. The old saying 'You can't teach an old dog new tricks' does not necessarily hold true, but it is true that it is much easier to discourage bad behaviour in a young developing pup than to wait until the pup's bad behaviour becomes the adult dog's bad habit. There are some problems that are especially prevalent in puppies as they develop.

NIPPING

As puppies start to teethe, they feel the need to sink their teeth into anything…including your fingers, arms, hair, and toes. You may find this behaviour cute for the first five seconds until you feel just how sharp those puppy teeth are. This is something you want to discourage immediately and consistently with a firm 'No!' (or whatever number of firm 'No's' it takes for him to understand that you mean business), then replace your finger with an appropriate chew toy. While this behaviour is merely annoying when the dog is young, it can become dangerous as your Dogue's adult teeth grow in and his jaws develop, if he thinks that it is okay to gnaw on human appendages. You do not want to take a chance with a Dogue as this is a breed whose jaws become very strong. He does not mean any harm with a friendly nip, but he does not know his own strength.

CRYING/WHINING

Your pup will often cry, whine, whimper, howl or make some type of commotion when he is left alone. This is his way of calling

> **DID YOU KNOW?**
> Chewing goes hand in hand with nipping in the sense that a teething puppy is always looking for a way to soothe his aching gums. In this case, instead of chewing on you, he may have taken a liking to your favourite shoe or something else which he should not be chewing. Again, realise that this is a normal canine behaviour that does not need to be discouraged, only redirected. Your pup just needs to be taught what is acceptable to chew on and what is off limits. Consistently tell him NO when you catch him chewing on something forbidden and give him a chew toy. Conversely, praise him when you catch him chewing on something appropriate. In this way you are discouraging the inappropriate behaviour and reinforcing the desired behaviour. The puppy chewing should stop after his adult teeth have come in, but an adult dog continues to chew for various reasons—perhaps because he is bored, perhaps to relieve tension or perhaps he just likes to chew. That is why it is important to redirect his chewing when he is still young.

out for attention to make sure that
you know he is there and that you
have not forgotten about him. He
feels insecure when he is left
alone: when you are out of the
house and he is in his crate, or
when you are in another part of
the house and he cannot see you.
The noise he is making is an
expression of the anxiety he feels
at being alone. He needs to be
taught that being alone is okay.
You are not actually training the
dog to stop making noise, you are
training him to feel comfortable
when he is alone and removing
the need for him to make noise.
When you are not there to
supervise, the puppy is safer in
his crate, filled with cosy blankets
and toys, than roaming freely
about the house. In order for the

pup to stay in his crate without
making a fuss, he needs to be
comfortable there. It is extremely
important that the crate is never
used as a form of punishment, or
the pup will have a negative
association with the crate.

Accustom the pup to the crate
in short, gradually increasing time
intervals in which you put him in
the crate, maybe with a treat, and
stay in the room with him. If he
cries or makes a fuss, do not go to
him, but stay in his sight.
Gradually he will realise that
staying in his crate is all right,
and it will not be so traumatic for
him when you are not around.
You may want to leave the radio
on softly when you leave the
house; the sound of human voices
may be comforting to him.

Your Dogue puppy will have been started on puppy food by the breeder. You should continue to feed your puppy this diet, and your vet will advise you of recommended dietary changes at the appropriate times.

DIETARY AND FEEDING CONSIDERATIONS

You have probably heard it a thousand times, 'you are what you eat.' Believe it or not, it's very true. Dogs are what you feed them because they have little choice in the matter. Even those people who truly want to feed their dogs the best often cannot do so because they do not know which foods are best for their dog.

Dog foods are produced in three basic types: dry, semi-moist and canned or tinned. Dry foods are for the cost conscious because they are much less expensive than semi-moist and canned. Dry foods contain the least fat and the most preservatives. Most tinned foods are 60–70-percent water, while semi-moist foods are so full of sugar that they are the least preferred by owners, though dogs welcome them (as a child does sweets).

Three stages of development must be considered when selecting a diet for your dog: the puppy stage, the mid-age or adult stage and the senior age or geriatric stage.

PUPPY STAGE

Puppies have a natural instinct to suck milk from their mother's breasts. They should exhibit this behaviour the first day of their lives. If they don't suckle within a few hours, you should attempt to put them onto their mother's nipple. If they fail to suckle, you have to feed them yourself under the advice and guidance of a veterinary surgeon. This will

DID YOU KNOW?
You must store your dry dog food carefully. Open packages of dog food quickly lose their vitamin value, usually within 90 days of being opened. Mould spores and vermin could also contaminate the food.

small portions of tinned meat after they are about one month old. Dry food is then gradually added to the mix.

By the time they are eight weeks old, they should be completely weaned and fed solely a puppy dry food. During this weaning period, diet is most important as the puppy grows

Puppies have a strong natural instinct for suckling. Their mother's milk is necessary for the first four weeks of their lives.

involve a baby bottle and a special formula. Their mother's milk is much better than any formula because it contains colostrum, an antibiotic milk that protects the puppy during the first eight to ten weeks of their lives.

Puppies should be allowed to nurse for six weeks and they should be slowly weaned away from their mother by introducing

DID YOU KNOW?
A good test for proper diet is the colour, odour, and firmness of your dog's stool. A healthy dog usually produces three semi-hard stools per day. The stools should have no unpleasant odour. They should be the same colour from excretion to excretion.

It is absolutely essential that your Dogue puppy receives proper nutrition in his first year, during his crucial growth period.

fastest during its first year of life. A Dogue de Bordeaux puppy will have a hearty appetite as soon as he becomes accustomed to his new home, and it is essential that he receives the best nutrition possible. If proper nutrition is not provided in the crucial growth stage of puppyhood, it may cause

Some dog owners like to cook for their dogs; however, it's usually easier to provide proper nutrition with a complete dog food than to try to figure out the right balance on your own.

deficiencies that cannot be made up for later in life. Never mistake proper nutrition for overfeeding. Young Dogue de Bordeaux puppies should not be allowed to eat beyond their own portions, paying special attention to avoiding table food. Excessive

weight on a Bordeaux pup can do irreparable harm to his growing joints. It's far better to have your Bordeaux slightly underweight than to fatten him up.

Puppy diets should be balanced for your dog's needs and supplements of vitamins, minerals and protein should not be necessary. Discuss supplements with your vet and breeder before offering any to your Dogue.

DID YOU KNOW?

Dog food must be at room temperature, neither too hot nor too cold. Fresh water, changed daily and served in a clean bowl, is mandatory, especially when feeding dry food.

Never feed your dog from the table while you are eating. Never feed your dog left-overs from your own meal. They usually contain too much fat and too much seasoning.

Dogs must chew their food. Hard pellets are excellent; soups and slurries are to be avoided.

Don't add left-overs or any extras to normal dog food. The normal food is usually balanced and adding something extra destroys the balance.

Except for age-related changes, dogs do not require dietary variations. They can be fed the same diet, day after day, without their becoming ill.

ADULT DIETS

A dog is considered an adult when it has stopped growing in height and/or length. Do not consider the dog's weight when making the decision to switch from a puppy diet to a maintenance diet. You should rely upon your veterinary surgeon to recommend an acceptable maintenance diet. Major dog food manufacturers specialise in this type of food and it is necessary for you to select the one best suited to your dog's needs. Active dogs may have different requirements than sedate dogs.

A Dogue de Bordeaux reaches adulthood at about two years of age, though some dogs may take up to three years.

DIETS FOR SENIOR DOGS

As dogs get older, their metabolism changes. The older dog usually exercises less, moves

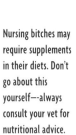

more slowly and sleeps more. This change in lifestyle and physiological performance requires a change in diet. Since these changes take place slowly, they might not be recognisable. What is easily recognisable is weight gain. Continually feeding your dog an adult maintenance diet when it is slowing down metabolically will cause him to gain weight. Obesity in an older dog compounds the health problems that already accompany old age.

As your dog gets older, few of his organs function up to par. The kidneys slow down and the intestines become less efficient. These age-related factors are best handled with a change in diet and a change in feeding schedule to

Nursing bitches may require supplements in their diets. Don't go about this yourself—always consult your vet for nutritional advice.

75

What are you feeding your dog?

Read the label on your dog food. Many dog foods only advise what 50—55% of the contents are, leaving the other 45% to doubt.

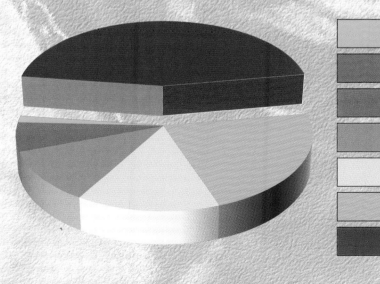

1.3% Calcium

1.6% Fatty Acids

4.6% Crude Fibre

11% Moisture

14% Crude Fat

22% Crude Protein

45.5% ? ? ?

give smaller portions that are more easily digested.

There is no single best diet for every older dog. While many dogs do well on light or senior diets, other dogs do better on puppy diets or other special premium diets such as lamb and rice. Be sensitive to your senior Dogue de Bordeaux's diet and this will help control other problems that may arise with your old friend.

WATER

Just as your dog needs proper nutrition from his food, water is an essential 'nutrient' as well. Water keeps the dog's body properly hydrated and promotes normal function of the body's systems. During housebreaking it is necessary to keep an eye on how much water your Dogue de Bordeaux is drinking, but once he is reliably trained he should have access to clean fresh water at all times. Make sure that the dog's water bowl is clean, and change the water often, making sure that water is always available for your dog, especially if you feed dried food.

EXERCISE

All dogs require some form of exercise, regardless of breed. A sedentary lifestyle is as harmful to a dog as it is to a person. The Dogue de Bordeaux happens to be an active breed that requires more exercise than, say, an English

Bulldog, but you don't have to be a weightlifter or marathon runner to provide your dog with the exercise he needs. Regular walks, play sessions in the garden, or letting the dog run free in the garden under your supervision are all sufficient forms of exercise for the Dogue de Bordeaux. For those who are more ambitious, you will find that your Dogue de Bordeaux will be able to keep up with you

'Have you got something there for me?' Some dogs are always looking for a treat!

on extra long walks or a morning run. Not only is exercise essential to keep the dog's body fit, it is essential to his mental well-being. A bored dog will find something to do, which often manifests itself in some type of destructive behaviour. In this sense, it is essential for the owner's mental well-being as well!

GROOMING
BRUSHING

A natural bristle brush or a slicker brush can be used for regular routine brushing. Daily brushing is effective for removing dead hair

77

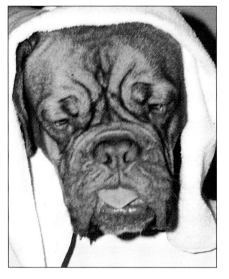

Bathing a Dogue de Bordeaux requires plenty of patience, time and towels! Don't forget to clean the facial wrinkles too.

and stimulating the dog's natural oils to add shine and a healthy look to the coat. Your Dogue de Bordeaux is not a breed that needs excessive grooming, but his heavy coat needs to be brushed daily as part of routine maintenance. Daily brushing will get rid of dust and dandruff and remove any dead hair. Regular grooming sessions are also a good way to spend time with your dog. Many dogs grow to like the feel of being brushed and enjoy the daily routine.

BATHING

Dogs do not need to be bathed as often as humans, but regular bathing is essential for healthy skin and a healthy, shiny coat. If you accustom your pup to being bathed as a puppy, it will be second nature by the time he grows up. You want your dog to

be at ease in the bath or it could end up a wet, soapy, messy ordeal for both of you!

Brush your Dogue de Bordeaux thoroughly before wetting his coat. Make sure that your dog has a good non-slip surface to stand on. Begin by wetting the dog's coat. A shower or hose attachment is necessary for thoroughly wetting and rinsing the coat. Check the water temperature to make sure that it is neither too hot nor too cold.

Next, apply shampoo to the dog's coat and work it into a good lather. You should purchase a shampoo that is made for dogs; do not use a product made for human hair. Wash the head last. You do

DID YOU KNOW?

How much grooming equipment you purchase will depend on how much grooming you are going to do. Here are some basics:

- Natural bristle brush
- Slicker brush
- Metal comb
- Scissors
- Blaster
- Rubber mat
- Dog shampoo
- Spray hose attachment
- Ear cleaner
- Cotton wipes
- Towels
- Nail clippers

Healthy dog hairs
enlarged about 500
times their natural
size. The inset shows
a growing tip.
Scanning electron
micrographs by Dr.
Dennis Kunkel,
University of Hawaii.

Your local pet shop will have a selection of grooming tools. Your Dogue will not require excessive grooming, but you'll want to have the basics handy for maintaining his short coat.

Once accustomed to it, your Dogue puppy will like being groomed with a soft brush or glove. Make it a daily routine.

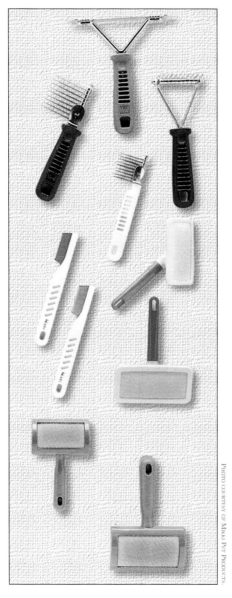

skin. You can use this opportunity to check the skin for any bumps, bites or other abnormalities. Do not neglect any area of the body— get all of the hard-to-reach places.

Once the dog has been thoroughly shampooed, he requires an equally thorough rinsing. Shampoo left in the coat can be irritating to the skin. Protect his eyes from the shampoo by shielding them with your hand

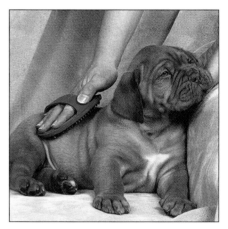

and directing the flow of water in the opposite direction. You should also avoid getting water in the ear canal. Be prepared for your dog to shake out his coat— you might want to stand back, but make sure you have a hold on the dog to keep him from running through the house.

EAR CLEANING
The ears should be kept clean and any excess hair inside the ear

not want shampoo to drip into the dog's eyes whilst you are washing the rest of his body. Work the shampoo all the way down to the

should be trimmed. Ears can be cleaned with a cotton bud and special cleaner or ear powder made especially for dogs. Be on the lookout for any signs of infection or ear mite infestation. If your Dogue de Bordeaux has been shaking his head or scratching at his ears frequently, this usually indicates a problem. If his ears have an unusual odour, this is a sure sign of mite infestation or infection, and a signal to have his ears checked by the veterinary surgeon.

DID YOU KNOW?

The use of human soap products like shampoo, bubble bath and hand soap can be damaging to a dog's coat and skin. Human products are too strong and remove the protective oils coating the dog's hair and skin (making him water-resistant). Use only shampoo made especially for dogs and you may like to use a medicated shampoo which will always help to keep external parasites at bay.

NAIL CLIPPING

Your Dogue de Bordeaux should be accustomed to having his nails trimmed at an early age, since it will be part of your maintenance routine throughout his life. Not only does it look nicer, but also a dog with long nails can cause injury if he jumps up or scratches

DID YOU KNOW?

Once you are sure that the dog is thoroughly rinsed, squeeze the excess water out of the coat with your hand and dry him with a heavy towel. You may choose to use a blaster on his coat or just let it dry naturally. In cold weather, never allow your dog outside with a wet coat.

There are 'dry bath' products on the market, which are sprays and powders intended for spot cleaning, that can be used between regular baths, if necessary. They are not substitutes for regular baths, but they are easy to use for touch-ups as they do not require rinsing.

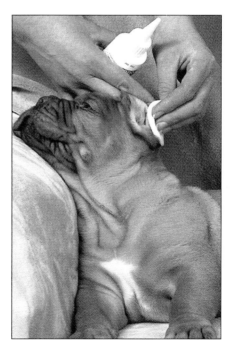

Your Dogue's ears should be checked and cleaned routinely. As you clean the ear with a proper cotton wipe and ear solution, be sure the ears are free of mites and any foul odour.

someone unintentionally. A long nail has a better chance of ripping and bleeding, or causing the feet to spread. If you can hear your dog's nails clicking on the floor when he walks, his nails are too long.

Before you start cutting, make sure you can identify the 'quick' in each nail. The quick is a blood vessel that runs through the centre of each nail and grows rather close to the end. It will bleed if accidentally cut, which will be quite painful for the dog as it contains nerve endings. Keep some type of clotting agent on hand, such as a styptic pencil or styptic powder (the type used for shaving). This will stop the bleeding quickly when applied to the end of the cut nail. Do not panic if you cut the quick, just

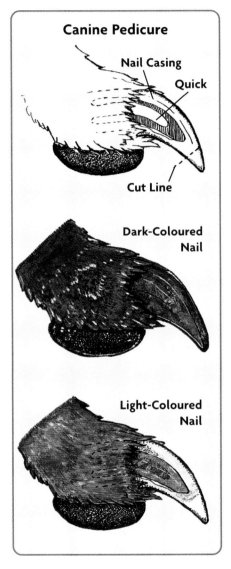

Canine Pedicure

Nail Casing

Quick

Cut Line

Dark-Coloured Nail

Light-Coloured Nail

DID YOU KNOW?

A dog that spends a lot of time outside on a hard surface such as cement or pavement will have his nails naturally worn down and may not need to have them trimmed as often, except maybe in the colder months when he is not outside as much. Regardless, it is best to get your dog accustomed to this procedure at an early age so that he is used to it. Some dogs are especially sensitive about having their feet touched, but if a dog has experienced it since he was young, he should not be bothered by it.

stop the bleeding and talk soothingly to your dog. Once he has calmed down, move on to the next nail. It is better to clip a little at a time, particularly with black-nailed dogs.

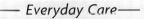

Hold your pup steady as you begin trimming his nails; you do not want him to make any sudden movements or run away. Talk to an early age. You may or may not often take him in the car, but he will need to go to the vet and you do not want these trips to be

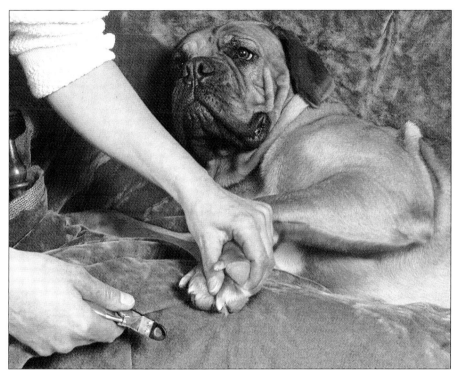

Clipping your dog's nails doesn't have to be an unpleasant experience. Usually dogs who have had their nails clipped since puppyhood are more tolerant of the experience.

him soothingly and stroke him as you clip. Hold his foot in your hand and simply take off the end of each nail in one quick clip. Nail clippers that are specially made for dogs can usually be found wherever you buy pet or grooming supplies.

TRAVELLING WITH YOUR DOG
CAR TRAVEL
You should accustom your Dogue de Bordeaux to riding in a car at traumatic for the dog or a big hassle for you. The safest way for a dog to ride in the car is in his crate. Wire crates can be used for travel, but fibreglass or wooden crates are safer. If he uses a fibreglass crate in the house, you can use the same crate for travel.

Put the pup in the crate and see how he reacts. If he seems uneasy, you can have a passenger hold him on his lap while you drive. Another option is a special-

83

ly made safety harness for dogs, which straps the dog in much like a seat belt. Do not let the dog roam loose in the vehicle—this is very dangerous! If you should stop short, your dog can be thrown and injured. If the dog starts climbing on you and pestering you while you are driving, you will not be able to concentrate on the road. It is an unsafe situation for everyone—human and canine.

take along some paper kitchen towels and perhaps some old towelling for use should he have an accident in the car or suffer from travel sickness.

Never allow your Dogue to travel in your car without being restrained. A crate will help keep your dog safe while travelling.

For long trips, be prepared to stop to let the dog relieve himself. Bring along whatever you need to clean up after him. You should

AIR TRAVEL
Whilst it is possible to take a dog on a flight within Britain, it is fairly unusual and advance permission is always required. The dog will be required to travel in a fibreglass crate and you should always check in advance with the airline regarding specific requirements. To help the dog be at ease, put one of his favourite toys in the crate with him. Do not feed the dog for at least six hours before the trip to minimise his need to relieve himself. However, certain regulations specify that water must always be made available to the dog in the crate.

Make sure your dog is properly identified and that your contact information appears on his ID tags

DID YOU KNOW?

However much your dog enjoys travelling, he should never be left alone in a car in warm weather, even with the windows left open. Heat builds up all too quickly and can cause suffering and tragedy. Even on a cloudy day one must always be aware that the sun can break through unexpectedly.

and on his crate. Animals travel in a different area of the plane than human passengers so every rule must be strictly adhered to so as to prevent the risk of getting separated from your dog.

BOARDING

So you want to take a family holiday—and you want to include all members of the family. You would probably make arrangements for accommodations ahead of time anyway, but this is especially important when travelling with a dog. You do not want to make an overnight stop at the only place

Your selection of a suitable boarding kennel should be based on location, cleanliness, the staff's knowledge, cost and activities for your Dogue.

DID YOU KNOW?

For international travel you will have to make arrangements well in advance (perhaps months), as countries' regulations pertaining to bringing in animals differ. There may be special health certificates and/or vaccinations that your dog will need before taking the trip, sometimes this has to be done within a certain time frame. In rabies-free countries, you will need to bring proof of the dog's rabies vaccination and there may be a quarantine period upon arrival.

around for miles and discover that they do not allow dogs. Also, you do not want to reserve a place for your family without mentioning that you are taking a dog, because if it is against their policy you may not have a place to stay.

Alternatively, if you are travelling and choose not to bring your Dogue de Bordeaux, you will have to make arrangements for him while you are away. Some options are to bring him to a neighbour's house to stay while you are gone, to have a trusted neighbour stop by often or stay at your house, or bring your dog to a reputable boarding kennel. If you choose to board him at a kennel, you should visit in advance to see the facility and where the dogs

DID YOU KNOW?

If your dog gets lost, he is not able to ask for directions home.

Identification tags fastened to the collar give important information—the dog's name, the owner's name, the owner's address and a telephone number where the owner can be reached. This makes it easy for whoever finds the dog to contact the owner and arrange to have the dog returned. An added advantage is that a person will be more likely to approach a lost dog who has ID tags on his collar; it tells the person that this is somebody's pet rather than a stray. This is the easiest and fastest method of identification provided that the tags stay on the collar and the collar stays on the dog.

DID YOU KNOW?

As puppies become more and more expensive, especially those puppies of high quality for showing and/or breeding, they have a greater chance of being stolen. The usual collar dog tag is, of course, easily removed. But there are two techniques that have become widely utilised for identification.

The puppy microchip implantation involves the injection of a small microchip, about the size of a corn kernel, under the skin of the dog. If your dog shows up at a clinic or shelter, or is offered for resale under less than savory circumstances, it can be positively identified by the microchip. The microchip is scanned and a registry quickly identifies you as the owner. This is not only protection against theft, but should the dog run away or go chasing a squirrel and get lost, you have a fair chance of getting it back.

Tattooing is done on various parts of the dog, from its belly to its cheeks. The number tattooed can be your telephone number or any other number which you can easily memorise. When professional dog thieves see a tattooed dog, they usually lose interest in it. Both microchipping and tattooing can be done at your local veterinary clinic. For the safety of our dogs, no laboratory facility or dog broker will accept a tattooed dog as stock.

are kept. Talk to some of the employees and see how they treat the dogs—do they spend time with the dogs, play with them, exercise them, etc.? Also find out the kennel's policy on vaccinations and what they require. This is for the safety of all the dogs. When dogs are kept together, there is a greater risk of diseases being passed from dog to dog.

IDENTIFICATION

Your Dogue de Bordeaux is your valued companion and friend. That is why you always keep a close eye on him and you have made sure that he cannot escape from the garden or wriggle out of his collar and run away from you. However, accidents can happen and there may come a time when your dog unexpectedly gets separated from you. If this unfortunate event should occur, the first thing on your mind will be finding him. Proper identification will increase the chances of his being returned to you safely and quickly.

Dogue de Bordeaux

Living with an untrained dog is a lot like owning a piano that you do not know how to play—it is a nice object to look at but it does not do much more than that to bring you pleasure. Now try taking piano lessons and suddenly the piano comes alive and brings forth magical sounds and rhythms that set your heart singing and your body swaying.

The same is true with your Dogue de Bordeaux. At first you enjoy seeing him around the house. He does not do much with you other than need food, water and exercise. Come to think of it, he does not bring you much joy, either. He is a big responsibility with a very small return. He may develop unacceptable behaviours that

annoy and/or infuriate you to say nothing of bad habits that may end up costing you great sums of money. Not a good thing!

Now train your Dogue de Bordeaux. Enrol in an obedience class. Teach him good manners as you learn how and why he behaves the way he does. Find

> **DID YOU KNOW?**
> Taking your dog to an obedience school may be the best investment in time and money you can ever make. You will enjoy the benefits for the lifetime of your dog and you will have the opportunity to meet people with your similar expectations for companion dogs.

> **DID YOU KNOW?**
> If you start with a normal, healthy dog and give him time, patience and some carefully executed lessons, you will reap the rewards of that training for the life of the dog. And what a life it will be! The two of you will find immeasurable pleasure in the companionship you have built together with love, respect and understanding. Good luck and enjoy!

out how to communicate with your dog and how to recognise and understand his communications with you. Suddenly the dog takes on a new role in your life— he is smart, interesting, well behaved and fun to be with. He demonstrates his bond of devotion to you daily. Your Dogue de Bordeaux does wonders for your ego because he constantly reminds you that you

Dogs gain much information through their acute sense of smell; this is how they find their relief area time and again.

are not only his leader, you are his hero! Miraculous things have happened—you have a wonderful dog (even your family and friends have noticed the transformation!) and you feel good about yourself.

Those involved with teaching dog obedience and counselling owners about their dogs' behaviour have discovered some interesting facts about dog ownership. For example, training dogs when they are puppies results in the highest rate of success in developing well-mannered and well-adjusted adult dogs. Training an older dog, from 6 months to 6 years of

age, can produce almost equal results providing that the owner accepts the dog's slower rate of learning capability and is willing to work patiently to help the dog succeed at developing to his fullest potential. Unfortunately,

DID YOU KNOW?

Training a dog is a life experience. Many parents admit that much of what they know about raising children they learned from caring for their dogs. Dogs respond to love, fairness and guidance, just as children do. Become a good dog owner and you may become an even better parent.

many owners of untrained adult dogs lack the patience factor, and do not persist until their dogs are successful at learning particular behaviours.

Training a puppy, aged 10 to 16 weeks (20 weeks at the most), is like working with a dry sponge in a pool of water. The pup soaks up whatever you show him and constantly looks for more things to do and learn. At this early age, his body is not yet producing hormones, and therein lies the reason for such a high rate of success. Without hormones, he is focused on his owners and not particularly interested in investigating other places, dogs, people, etc. You are his leader; his provider of food, water, shelter and security. Therefore, he latches onto you and wants to stay close. He will usually follow you from room to room, will not let you out of his sight when you

DID YOU KNOW?

Dogs are sensitive to their master's moods and emotions. Use your voice wisely when communicating with your dog. Never raise your voice at your dog unless you are angry and trying to correct him. 'Barking' at your dog can become as meaningless as 'dogspeak' is to you. Think before you bark!

are outdoors with him, and responds in like manner to the people and animals you encounter. If you greet a friend warmly, he will be happy to greet the person as well. If, however, you are hesitant, even anxious, about the approach of a stranger, he will respond accordingly.

Once the puppy begins to produce hormones, his natural curiosity emerges and he begins to investigate the world around him. It is at that time when you may notice that the untrained dog begins to wander away from you and even ignore your commands to stay close. When this behaviour becomes a problem, there is no option except to train the dog!

Occasionally there are no classes available within a reasonable distance from the owner's home. Sometimes there are classes available but the tuition is too costly. Whatever the circumstances, the solution to

DID YOU KNOW?

Mealtime should be a peaceful time for your puppy. Do not put his food and water bowls in a high-traffic area in the house. For example, give him his own little corner of the kitchen where he can eat undisturbed and where he will not be under foot. Do not allow small children or other family members to disrupt the pup when he is eating.

the problem of lack of lesson availability lies within the pages of this book. You can do much to train the dog yourself. This chapter is devoted to helping you train your Dogue de Bordeaux at home. If the recommended procedures are followed faithfully, you may expect positive results that will prove rewarding to both you and your dog.

Whether your Dogue de Bordeaux is a puppy or a mature adult, the methods of teaching and the techniques we use in training basic behaviours are the same. After all, no dog, whether puppy or adult, likes harsh or inhumane methods. All creatures, however, respond favourably to gentle motivational methods and sincere praise and encouragement. Now let us get started.

HOUSEBREAKING

You can train a puppy to relieve itself wherever you choose, but this must be somewhere suitable. You should bear in mind from the outset that when your puppy is old enough to go out in public places, any canine deposits must be removed at once. You will always have to carry with you a small plastic bag or 'poop scoop.' City dwellers often train their puppies to relieve themselves in the gutter because large plots of grass are not readily available. Suburbanites, on the other hand,

usually have gardens to accommodate their dogs' needs.

Outdoor training includes such surfaces as grass, dirt and cement. Indoor training usually means training your dog to newspaper.

When deciding on the surface and location that you will want your Dogue de Bordeaux to use, be sure it is going to be permanent. Training your dog to grass and then changing your mind two months later is extremely difficult for both dog and owner.

Next, choose the command you will use each and every time you want your puppy to void. 'Go hurry up' and 'Toilet' are examples of commands commonly used by dog owners.

Get in the habit of giving the puppy your chosen relief command before you take him out. That way, when he becomes

DID YOU KNOW?
To a dog's way of thinking, your hands are like his mouth in terms of a defence mechanism. If you squeeze him too tightly, he might just bite you because that would be his normal response. This is not aggressive biting and, although all biting should be discouraged, you need the discipline in learning how to handle your dog.

an adult, you will be able to determine if he wants to go out when you ask him. A confirmation will be signs of interest, wagging his tail, watching you intently, going to the door, etc.

PUPPY'S NEEDS
Puppy needs to relieve himself after play periods, after each meal, after he has been sleeping

---

HOW MANY TIMES A DAY?

AGE	RELIEF TRIPS
To 14 weeks	10
14–22 weeks	8
22–32 weeks	6
Adulthood	4
(dog stops growing)	

These are estimates, of course, but they are a guide to the MINIMUM opportunities a dog should have each day to relieve itself.

---

and any time he indicates that he is looking for a place to urinate or defecate.

The urinary and intestinal tract muscles of very young puppies are not fully developed. Therefore, like human babies, puppies need to relieve themselves frequently.

Take your puppy out often—every hour for an eight-week-old, for example, and always immediately after feeding or sleeping.

The older the puppy, the less often he will need to relieve himself. Finally, as a mature healthy adult, he will require only three to five relief trips per day.

HOUSING
Since the types of housing and control you provide for your puppy has a direct relationship on the success of housetraining, we consider the various aspects of both before we begin training.

Bringing a new puppy home and turning him loose in your house can be compared to turning a child loose in a sports arena and telling the child that the place is all his! The sheer enormity of the place would be too much for him to handle.

Instead, offer the puppy clearly defined areas where he can play, sleep, eat and live. A room of the house where the

---

DID YOU KNOW?
Dogs will do anything for your attention. If you reward the dog when he is calm and resting, you will develop a well-mannered dog. If, on the other hand, you greet your dog excitedly and encourage him to wrestle and roughhouse with you, the dog will greet you the same way and you will have a hyper dog on your hands.

Canine Development Schedule

It is important to understand how and at what age a puppy develops into adulthood. If you are a puppy owner, consult the following Canine Development Schedule to determine the stage of development your Dogue de Bordeaux puppy is currently experiencing. This knowledge will help you as you work with the puppy in the weeks and months ahead.

Period	Age	Characteristics
FIRST TO THIRD	BIRTH TO SEVEN WEEKS	Puppy needs food, sleep and warmth, and responds to simple and gentle touching. Needs mother for security and disciplining. Needs littermates for learning and interacting with other dogs. Pup learns to function within a pack and learns pack order of dominance. Begin socialising with adults and children for short periods. Begins to become aware of its environment.
FOURTH	EIGHT TO TWELVE WEEKS	Brain is fully developed. Needs socialising with outside world. Remove from mother and littermates. Needs to change from canine pack to human pack. Human dominance necessary. Fear period occurs between 8 and 16 weeks. Avoid fright and pain.
FIFTH	THIRTEEN TO SIXTEEN WEEKS	Training and formal obedience should begin. Less association with other dogs, more with people, places, situations. Period will pass easily if you remember this is pup's change-to-adolescence time. Be firm and fair. Flight instinct prominent. Permissiveness and over-disciplining can do permanent damage. Praise for good behaviour.
JUVENILE	FOUR TO EIGHT MONTHS	Another fear period about 7 to 8 months of age. It passes quickly, but be cautious of fright and pain. Sexual maturity reached. Dominant traits established. Dog should understand sit, down, come and stay by now.

NOTE: THESE ARE APPROXIMATE TIME FRAMES. ALLOW FOR INDIVIDUAL DIFFERENCES IN PUPPIES.

From housebreaking to basic commands to teaching manners, you shape your puppy's behaviour from the moment you bring him home.

family gathers is the most obvious choice. Puppies are social animals and need to feel a part of the pack right from the start. Hearing your voice, watching you while you are doing things and smelling you nearby are all positive reinforcers that he is now a member of your pack. Usually a family room, the kitchen or a nearby adjoining breakfast area is ideal for providing safety and security for both puppy and owner.

Within that room there should be a smaller area which the puppy can call his own. An alcove, a wire or fibreglass dog crate or a fenced (not boarded!) corner from which he can view the activities of his new family will be fine. The size of the area or crate is the key factor here. The area must be large enough for the puppy to lie down and stretch out as well as stand up without rubbing his head on the top, yet small enough so that he cannot relieve himself at one end and sleep at the other without coming into contact with his droppings until fully trained to relieve himself outside.

Dogs are, by nature, clean animals and will not remain close to their relief areas unless forced to do so. In those cases, they become dirty dogs and usually remain that way for life.

The crate or cubby should be lined with a clean bedding and

TRAINING TIP

Stand up straight and authoritatively when giving your dog commands. Do not issue commands when lying on the floor or lying on your back on the sofa. If you are on your hands and knees when you give a command, your dog will think you are positioning yourself to play.

offer one toy, no more. Do not put food or water in the crate, as eating and drinking will activate his digestive processes and ultimately defeat your purpose as well as make the puppy very uncomfortable as he attempts to 'hold it.'

CONTROL

By control, we mean helping the puppy to create a lifestyle pattern that will be compatible to that of his human pack (YOU!). Just as we guide little children to learn our way of life, we must show the puppy when it is time to play, eat, sleep, exercise and even entertain himself.

Your puppy should always sleep in his crate. He should also learn that, during times of household confusion and excessive human activity such as at breakfast when family members are preparing for the day, he can play by himself in relative safety and comfort in his crate. Each time you leave the

puppy alone, he should be crated. Puppies are chewers. They cannot tell the difference between lamp cords, television wires, shoes, table legs, etc. Chewing into a television wire can be fatal to the puppy while a shorted wire can start a fire in the house.

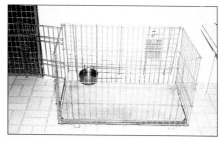

Housing is a big part of training your dog. Your Dogue will not want to soil where he sleeps and will usually need to relieve himself after spending a period of time in his crate.

If the puppy chews on the arm of the chair when he is alone, you will probably discipline him angrily when you

DID YOU KNOW?

Never line your pup's sleeping area with newspaper. Puppy litters are usually raised on newspaper and, once in your home, the puppy will immediately associate newspaper with voiding. Never put newspaper on any floor while housetraining, as this will only confuse the puppy. If you are paper-training him, use paper in his designated relief area ONLY. Finally, restrict water intake after evening meals. Offer a few licks at a time—never let a young puppy gulp water after meals.

get home. Thus, he makes the association that your coming home means he is going to be punished. (He will not remember chewing up the chair and is incapable of making the association of the discipline with his naughty deed.)

Purchase equipment for cleaning up after your dog. The easier it is for you, the more likely you are to do it!

Other times of excitement, such as family parties, etc., can be fun for the puppy providing he can view the activities from the security of his crate. He is not underfoot and he is not being fed all sorts of titbits that will probably cause him stomach distress, yet he still feels a part of the fun.

TRAINING TIP
The golden rule of dog training is simple. For each 'question' (command), there is only one correct answer (reaction). One command = one reaction. Keep practising the command until the dog reacts correctly without hesitating. Be repetitive but not monotonous. Dogs get bored just as people do!

TRAINING TIP
Practice Makes Perfect!
• Have training lessons with your dog every day in several short segments—three to five times a day for a few minutes at a time is ideal.
• Do not have long practice sessions. The dog will become easily bored.
• Never practice when you are tired, ill, worried or in an otherwise negative mood. This will transmit to the dog and may have an adverse effect on its performance.
   Think fun, short and above all POSITIVE! End each session on a high note, rather than a failed exercise, and make sure to give a lot of praise. Enjoy the training and help your dog enjoy it, too.

SCHEDULE
A puppy should be taken to his relief area each time he is released from his crate, after meals, after a play session, when he first awakens in the morning (at eight weeks, this can mean 5 am!) and whenever he indicates by circling or sniffing busily that he needs to urinate or defecate. For a puppy less than ten weeks of age, a routine of taking him out every hour is necessary. As the puppy grows, he will be able to wait for longer periods of time.
   Keep trips to his relief area short. Stay no more than five or six minutes and then return to the house. If he goes during that time, praise him lavishly and

TRAINING TIP

Most of all, be consistent. Always take your dog to the same location, always use the same command, and always have him on lead when he is in his relief area, unless a fenced-in garden is available.

By following the Success Method, your puppy will be completely housetrained by the time his muscle and brain development reach maturity. Keep in mind that small breeds usually mature faster than large breeds, but all puppies should be trained by six months of age.

Training your Dogue de Bordeaux should be taken very seriously. An untrained dog, especially one of this size, can cause quite a bit of trouble.

take him indoors immediately. If he does not, but he has an accident when you go back indoors, pick him up immediately, say 'No! No!' and return to his relief area. Wait a few minutes, then return to the house again. NEVER hit a puppy or rub his face in urine or excrement when he has an accident!

Once indoors, put the puppy in his crate until you have had time to clean up his accident. Then release him to the family area and watch him more closely than before. Chances are, his accident was a result of your not picking up his signal or waiting too long before offering him the opportunity to relieve himself. NEVER hold a grudge against the puppy for accidents.

Let the puppy learn that going outdoors means it is time to relieve himself, not play. Once trained, he will be able to play indoors and out and still differentiate between the times for play versus the times for relief.

Help him develop regular hours for naps, being alone, playing by himself and just resting, all in his crate. Encourage him to entertain himself while you are busy with

TRAINING TIP

Do not carry your dog to his toilet area. Lead him there on a leash or, better yet, encourage him to follow you to the spot. If you start carrying him to his spot, you might end up doing this routine forever and your dog will have the satisfaction of having trained YOU.

THE SUCCESS METHOD
6 Steps to Successful Crate Training

1 Tell the puppy 'Crate time!' and place him in the crate with a small treat (a piece of cheese or half of a biscuit). Let him stay in the crate for five minutes while you are in the same room. Then release him and praise lavishly. Never release him when he is fussing. Wait until he is quiet before you let him out.

2 Repeat Step 1 several times a day.

3 The next day, place the puppy in the crate as before. Let him stay there for ten minutes. Do this several times.

4 Continue building time in five-minute increments until the puppy stays in his crate for 30 minutes with you in the room. Always take him to his relief area after prolonged periods in his crate.

5 Now go back to Step 1 and let the puppy stay in his crate for five minutes, this time while you are out of the room.

6 Once again, build crate time in five-minute increments with you out of the room. When the puppy will stay willingly in his crate (he may even fall asleep!) for 30 minutes with you out of the room, he will be ready to stay in it for several hours at a time.

your activities. Let him learn that having you near is comforting, but it is not your main purpose in life to provide him with undivided attention.

Each time you put a puppy in his crate tell him, 'Crate time!' (or whatever command you choose). Soon, he will run to his crate when he hears you say those words.

In the beginning of his training, do not leave him in his crate for prolonged periods of time except during the night when everyone is sleeping. Make his experience with his crate a pleasant one and, as an adult, he will love his crate and willingly stay in it for several hours. There are millions of people who go to work every day and leave their adult dogs crated while they are away. The dogs accept this as their lifestyle and look forward to 'crate time.'

Crate training provides safety for you, the puppy and the home. It also provides the puppy with a feeling of security, and that helps the puppy achieve self-confidence and clean habits.

Remember that one of the primary ingredients in

Your housetrained Dogue will let you know when he needs to go out...listen to him! Fully-grown dogs should be able to control their urges for about six hours at a time, usually longer during the night.

of 'accidents' and ready to move on to a full and rewarding life together.

ROLES OF DISCIPLINE, REWARD AND PUNISHMENT

Discipline, training one to act in accordance with rules, brings order to life. It is as simple as that. Without discipline, particularly in a group society, chaos reigns supreme and the group will eventually perish. Humans and canines are social animals and need some form of discipline in order to function effectively. They must procure food, protect their home base and their young and reproduce to keep the species going.

If there were no discipline in the lives of social animals, they would eventually die from starvation and/or predation by other stronger animals.

In the case of domestic canines, dogs need discipline in

housetraining your puppy is control. Regardless of your lifestyle, there will always be occasions when you will need to have a place where your dog can stay and be happy and safe. Despite the reservations of the unenlightened, crate training is the answer for now and the future.

In conclusion, a few key elements are really all you need for a successful house and crate training method—consistency, frequency, praise, control and supervision. By following these procedures with a normal, healthy puppy, you and the puppy will soon be past the stage

DID YOU KNOW?
Success that comes by luck is usually short lived. Success that comes by well-thought-out proven methods is often more easily achieved and permanent. This is the Success Method. It is designed to give you, the puppy owner, a simple yet proven way to help your puppy develop clean living habits and a feeling of security in his new environment.

99

their lives in order to understand how their pack (you and other family members) functions and how they must act in order to survive.

A large humane society in a highly populated area recently surveyed dog owners regarding their satisfaction with their relationships with their dogs. People who had trained their dogs were 75% more satisfied with their pets than those who had never trained their dogs.

Dr. Edward Thorndike, a psychologist, established *Thorndike's Theory of Learning,* which states that a behaviour that results in a pleasant event tends to be repeated. A behaviour that results in an unpleasant event tends not to be repeated. Today's training methods are based on this theory.

TRAINING TIP
Dogs are as different from each other as people are. What works for one dog may not work for another. Have an open mind. If one method of training is unsuccessful, try another.

For example, if you manipulate a dog to perform a specific behaviour and reward him for doing it, he is likely to do it again because he enjoyed the end result.

Occasionally, punishment, a penalty inflicted for an offence, is necessary. The best type of punishment often comes from an outside source. For example, a child is told not to touch the stove because he may get burned. He disobeys and touches the stove. In doing so, he receives a burn. From that time on, he respects the heat of the stove and avoids contact with it. Therefore, a behaviour that results in an unpleasant event tends not to be repeated.

A good example of a dog learning the hard way is the dog that chases the house cat. He is told many times to leave the cat alone, yet he persists in teasing the cat. Then, one day he begins chasing the cat but the cat turns and swipes a claw across the dog's face, leaving him with a

DID YOU KNOW?
The puppy should also have regular play and exercise sessions when he is with you or a family member. Exercise for a very young puppy can consist of a short walk around the house or garden. Playing can include fetching games with a large ball or a special raggy. (All puppies teethe and need soft things upon which to chew.) Remember to restrict play periods to indoors within his living area (the family room for example) until he is completely housetrained.

TRAINING TIP

Do not use a choke collar on a dog under four months of age. Choke collars are for training only and should be removed after the lessons or exercises.

painful gash on his nose. The final result is that the dog stops chasing the cat.

TRAINING EQUIPMENT
COLLAR
A simple buckle collar is fine for most dogs. One who pulls mightily on the leash may require a chain choker collar. Only in the most severe cases of a dog being totally out of control is a prong or pinch collar recommended, and then only if the owner has been instructed in the proper use of such equipment. In some areas, such as the United Kingdom, these types of collars are not allowed.

LEAD
A 1- to 2-metre lead is recommended, preferably made of leather, nylon or heavy cloth. A chain lead is not recommended, as many dog owners find that the chain cuts into their hands and that switching the lead back and forth frequently between their hands is painful.

TREATS
Have a bag of treats on hand. Something nutritious and easy to swallow works best; use a soft treat, a chunk of cheese or a piece of cooked chicken rather than a dry biscuit. By the time the dog gets done chewing a dry treat, he will forget why he is

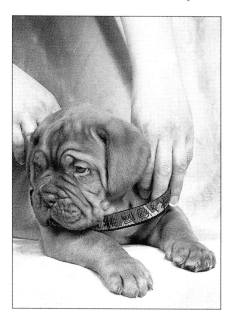

A simple buckle collar is sufficient for your Dogue puppy. Identification tags should be attached to the collar.

TRAINING TIP

If you want to be successful in training your dog, you have four rules to obey yourself:
1. Develop an understanding of how a dog thinks.
2. Do not blame the dog for lack of communication.
3. Define your dog's personality and act accordingly.
4. Have patience and be consistent.

being rewarded in the first place! Using food rewards will not teach a dog to beg at the table— the only way to teach a dog to beg at the table is to give him food from the table. In training, rewarding the dog with a food treat will help him associate praise and the treats with learning new behaviours that obviously please his owner.

TRAINING BEGINS: ASK THE DOG A QUESTION

In order to teach your dog, you must first get his attention. He cannot learn anything if he is looking away from you with his mind on something else.

To get his attention, ask him, 'School?' and immediately walk over to him and give him a treat as you tell him 'Good dog.' Wait a minute or two and repeat the routine, this time with a treat in your hand as you approach within a foot of the dog. Do not go directly to him, but stop about a foot away and hold out the treat as you ask, 'School?' He will see you approaching with a treat in your hand and most likely begin

> **TRAINING TIP**
> Never train your dog, puppy or adult, when you are mad or in a sour mood. Dogs are very sensitive to human feelings, especially anger, and if your dog senses that you are angry or upset, he will connect your anger with his training and learn to resent or fear his training sessions.

walking toward you. As you meet, give him the treat and praise again.

The third time, ask the question, have a treat in your hand and walk only a short distance toward the dog so that he must walk almost all the way to you. As he reaches you, give him the treat and praise again.

By this time, the dog will probably be getting the idea that if he pays attention to you, especially when you ask that question, it will pay off in treats and fun activities for him. In other words, he learns that 'school' means doing fun things with you that result in treats and positive attention for him.

Remember that the dog does not understand your verbal language, he only recognises sounds. Your question translates to a series of sounds for him, and those sounds become the signal to go to you and pay attention. If he does, he will get to interact with you plus receive treats and praise.

> **TRAINING TIP**
> Use treats to bribe your dog into a desired behaviour. Try small pieces of hard cheese or freeze-dried liver. Never offer chocolate as it has toxic qualities for dogs

'Good dog! Good sit!,' etc. Always remember to praise enthusiastically. Dogs relish verbal praise from their owners and feel so proud of themselves whenever they accomplish a behaviour.

You will not use food forever in getting the dog to obey your commands. Food is only used to teach new behaviours, and once the dog knows what you want when you give a specific command, you will wean him off the food treats but maintain the verbal praise. After all, you will always have your voice with you, but there will be many times when you have no food rewards yet expect the dog to obey.

It is much easier to teach a Dogue puppy than a full-grown Dogue. Not only do pups learn faster but it is also very difficult physically to guide a dog of this size into the desired positions.

THE BASIC COMMANDS
TEACHING SIT

Now that you have the dog's attention, hold the lead in your left hand and the food treat in your right. Place your food hand at the dog's nose and let him lick the treat but not take it from you. Say 'Sit' and slowly raise your food hand from in front of the dog's nose up over his head so that he is looking at the ceiling. As he bends his head upward, he will have to bend his knees to maintain his balance. As he bends his knees, he will assume a sit position. At that point, release the food treat and praise lavishly with comments such as

TEACHING DOWN

Teaching the down exercise is easy when you understand how the dog perceives the down

DID YOU KNOW?
Dogs do not understand our language. They can be trained to react to a certain sound, at a certain volume. If you say 'No, Oliver' in a very soft pleasant voice it will not have the same meaning as 'No, Oliver!!' when you shout it as loud as you can. You should never use the dog's name during a reprimand, just the command NO!! Since dogs don't understand words, comics use dogs trained with opposite meanings. Thus, when the comic commands his dog to SIT the dog will stand up; and vice versa.

Teaching the Down command requires that the owner understand that most dogs do not appreciate being in a submissive position. You may have to assist your Dogue into the appropriate position.

position, and it is very difficult when you do not. Dogs perceive the down position as a submissive posture. In addition, teaching the down exercise using the wrong method can sometimes make the dog develop such a fear of the down that he either runs away when you say

'down' or attempts to snap at the person who tries to force him down.

Have the dog sit close along side your left leg, facing in the same direction as you are. Hold the lead in your left hand and a food treat in your right. Now place your left hand lightly on the top of the dog's shoulders where they meet above the spinal cord. Do not push down on the dog's shoulders; simply rest your left hand there so you can guide the dog to lie down close to your left leg rather than to swing away from your side when he drops.

Now place the food hand at the dog's nose, say 'Down' very softly (almost a whisper), and slowly lower the food hand to the dog's front feet. When the food hand reaches the floor, begin moving it forward along the floor in front of the dog. Keep talking softly to the dog, saying things like, 'Do you want this treat? You can do this, good dog.' Your reassuring tone of voice will help calm the dog as he tries

TRAINING TIP

Play fetch games with your puppy in an enclosed area where he can retrieve his toy and bring it back to you. Always use a toy or object designated just for this purpose. Never use a shoe, sock or other item he may later confuse with those in your closet or underneath your chair.

It is not difficult to teach your Dogue to stay when he understands what is expected of him. Practice makes perfect.

to follow the food hand in order to get the treat.

When the dog's elbows touch the floor, release the food and praise softly. Try to get the dog to maintain that down position for several seconds before you let him sit up again. The goal here is to get the dog to settle down and not feel threatened in the down position.

DID YOU KNOW?

By providing sleeping and resting quarters that fit the dog, and offering frequent opportunities to relieve himself outside his quarters, the puppy quickly learns that the outdoors (or the newspaper if you are training him to paper) is the place to go when he needs to urinate or defecate. It also reinforces his innate desire to keep his sleeping quarters clean. This, in turn, helps develop the muscle control that will eventually produce a dog with clean living habits.

TEACHING STAY

It is easy to teach the dog to stay in either a sit or a down position. Again, we use food and praise during the teaching process as we help the dog to understand exactly what it is that we are expecting him to do.

To teach the sit/stay, start with the dog sitting on your left side as before and hold the lead in your left hand. Have a food treat in your right hand and place your food hand at the dog's nose. Say 'Stay' and step out on your right foot to stand directly in front of the dog, toe to toe, as he licks and nibbles the treat. Be sure to keep his head facing upward to maintain the sit position. Count to five and then swing around to stand next to the dog again with him on your left. As soon as you get back to the original position, release the food and praise lavishly.

To teach the down/stay, do the down as previously described. As soon as the dog lies down, say 'Stay' and step out on your right foot just as you did in the sit/stay. Count to five and then return to stand beside the dog with him on your left side. Release the treat and praise as always.

Within a week or ten days, you can begin to add a bit of distance between you and your dog when you leave him. When you do, use your left hand open with the palm facing the dog as a

stay signal, much the same as the hand signal a police officer uses to stop traffic at an intersection. Hold the food treat in your right hand as before, but this time the food is not touching the dog's nose. He will watch the food hand and quickly learn that he is going to get that treat as soon as you return to his side.

When you can stand one metre away from your dog for 30 seconds, you can then begin building time and distance in both stays. Eventually, the dog can be expected to remain in the stay position for prolonged periods of time until you return to him or call him to you. Always praise lavishly when he stays.

TEACHING COME
If you make teaching 'Come' a fun experience, you should never have a 'student' that does not love the game or that fails to

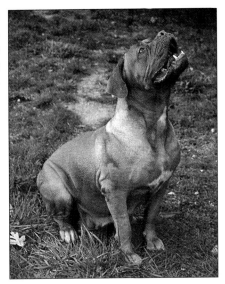

A well-trained Dogue will sit/stay, but he will be eagerly awaiting your COME signal.

come when called. The secret, it seems, is never to teach the word 'Come.'

At times when an owner most wants his dog to come when called, the owner is likely upset or anxious and he allows these feelings to come through in the tone of his voice when he calls his dog. Hearing that desperation in his owner's voice, the dog fears the results of going to him and therefore either disobeys or runs in the opposite direction. The secret, therefore, is to teach the dog a game and, when you want him to come to you, simply play the game. It is practically a no-fail solution!

To begin, have several members of your family take a few food treats and each go into a different room in the house. Take turns calling the dog. Each person should celebrate the dog's finding him with a treat and lots of happy praise. When a person calls the dog, he is actually

How about a handshake...or a 'pawshake'? Training doesn't always have to be serious. Dogues can be taught to do fun things too!

inviting the dog to find him and get a treat as a reward for 'winning.'

A few turns of the 'Where are you?' game and the dog will figure out that everyone is playing the game and that each person has a big celebration awaiting his success at locating them. Once he learns to love the game, simply calling out 'Where are you?' will bring him running from wherever he is when he hears that all-important question.

The come command is recognised as one of the most important things to teach a dog, so it is interesting to note that there are trainers who work with thousands of dogs and never teach the actual word 'Come.' Yet these dogs will race to respond

---

TRAINING TIP

When calling the dog, do not say 'Come.' Say things like, 'Rover, where are you? See if you can find me! I have a cookie for you!' Keep up a constant line of chatter with coaxing sounds and frequent questions such as, 'Where are you?' The dog will learn to follow the sound of your voice to locate you and receive his reward.

HEEL is not just a necessary command for the show ring. Every Dogue must learn to walk politely on the lead for everyday walks.

to a person who uses the dog's name followed by 'Where are you?' In one instance, a woman had a 12-year-old companion dog who went blind, but who never failed to locate her owner when asked, 'Where are you?'

Children particularly love to play this game with their dogs. Children can hide in smaller places like a shower or bathtub, behind a bed or under a table. The dog needs to work a little bit harder to find these hiding places, but when he does he loves to celebrate with a treat and a tussle with a favourite youngster.

TEACHING HEEL

Heeling means that the dog walks beside the owner without pulling. It takes time and patience on the owner's part to succeed at teaching the dog that he (the owner) will not proceed unless the dog is walking calmly beside him. Pulling out ahead on the lead is definitely not acceptable.

Begin with holding the lead in your left hand as the dog sits beside your left leg. Hold the loop end of the lead in your right hand but keep your left hand short on the lead so it keeps the dog in close next to you.

TRAINING TIP

If you begin teaching the heel by taking long walks and letting the dog pull you along, he misinterprets this action as an acceptable form of taking a walk. When you pull back on the lead to counteract his pulling, he reads that tug as a signal to pull even harder!

Say 'Heel' and step forward on your left foot. Keep the dog close to you and take three steps. Stop and have the dog sit next to you in what we now call the 'heel position.' Praise verbally, but do not touch the dog. Hesitate a moment and begin again with 'Heel,' taking three steps and stopping, at which point the dog is told to sit again.

Your goal here is to have the dog walk those three steps without pulling on the lead. When he will walk calmly beside you for three steps without pulling, increase the number of steps you take to five. When he will walk politely beside you while you take five steps, you can increase the length of your walk to ten steps. Keep increasing the length of your stroll until the dog will walk quietly beside you without pulling as long as you want him to heel. When you stop heeling, indicate to the dog that the exercise is over by verbally praising as you pet him and say 'OK, good dog.' The 'OK' is used as a release word

meaning that the exercise is finished and the dog is free to relax.

If you are dealing with a dog who insists on pulling you around, simply 'put on your brakes' and stand your ground until the dog realises that the two of you are not going anywhere until he is beside you and moving at your pace, not his. It may take some time just standing there to convince the dog that you are the leader and you will be the one to decide on the direction and speed of your travel.

Each time the dog looks up at you or slows down to give a slack lead between the two of you, quietly praise him and say, 'Good heel. Good dog.' Eventually, the dog will begin to respond and within a few days he will be walking politely beside you without pulling on the lead. At first, the training sessions should be kept short and very positive; soon the dog will be able to walk nicely with you for increasingly longer

TRAINING TIP

Teach your dog to HEEL in an enclosed area. Once you think the dog will obey reliably and you want to attempt advanced obedience exercises such as off-lead heeling, test him in a fenced in area so he cannot run away.

distances. Remember also to give the dog free time and the opportunity to run and play when you are done with heel practice.

WEANING OFF FOOD IN TRAINING

Food is used in training new behaviours, yet once the dog understands what behaviour goes with a specific command, it is time to start weaning him off the food treats. At first, give a treat after each exercise. Then, start to give a treat only after every other exercise. Mix up the times when you offer a food reward and the times when you only offer praise so that the dog will never know when he is going to receive both food and praise and when he is going to receive only praise. This is called a variable ratio reward system and it proves successful because there is always the chance that the owner will produce a treat, so the dog never stops trying for that reward. No matter what, ALWAYS give verbal praise.

OBEDIENCE CLASSES

As previously discussed, it is a good idea to enrol in an obedience class if one is available in your area. Many areas have dog clubs that offer basic obedience training as well as preparatory classes for obedience competition. There are also local dog trainers who offer similar classes.

At obedience trials, dogs can earn titles at various levels of competition. The beginning levels of competition include basic behaviours such as sit, down, heel, etc. The more advanced levels of competition include jumping, retrieving, scent discrimination and signal work. The advanced levels require a dog and owner to put a lot of time and effort into their training, and the titles that can be earned at these levels of competition are very prestigious.

OTHER ACTIVITIES FOR LIFE

Whether a dog is trained in the structured environment of a class or alone with his owner at home, there are many activities that can bring fun and rewards to both owner and dog once they have mastered basic control.

DID YOU KNOW?
A basic obedience beginner's class usually lasts for six to eight weeks. Dog and owner attend an hour-long lesson once a week and practice for a few minutes, several times a day, each day at home. If done properly, the whole procedure will result in a well-mannered dog and an owner who delights in living with a pet that is eager to please and enjoys doing things with his owner.

Teaching the dog to help out around the home, in the garden or on the farm provides great satisfaction to both dog and owner. In addition, the dog's help makes life a little easier for his owner and raises his stature as a valued companion to his family. It helps give the dog a purpose; it helps to keep his mind occupied and provides an outlet for his energy.

Backpacking is an exciting and healthy activity that the dog can be taught without assistance from more than his owner. The exercise of walking and climbing is good for man and dog alike, and the bond that they develop together is priceless.

If you are interested in participating in organised competition with your Dogue de Bordeaux, there are activities other than obedience in which you and your dog can become involved. Agility is a popular and fun sport where dogs run through an obstacle course that includes various jumps, tunnels and other exercises to test the dog's speed and coordination. The owners run through the course beside their dogs to give commands and to guide them through the course. Although competitive, the focus is on fun—it's fun to do and fun to watch, as well as great exercise.

As a Dogue de Bordeaux owner, you have the opportunity to participate in Schutzhund

DID YOU KNOW?

Occasionally, a dog and owner who have not attended formal classes have been able to earn entry-level titles by obtaining competition rules and regulations from a local kennel club and practising on their own to a degree of perfection. Obtaining the higher level titles, however, almost always requires extensive training under the tutelage of experienced instructors. In addition, the more difficult levels require more specialised equipment whereas the lower levels do not.

competition if you choose. Schutzhund originated as a test to determine the best quality German Shepherds to be used for breeding stock. Now it is open to all breeds, and it is used as a way to evaluate working ability and temperament. There are three levels of Schutzhund: SchH. I, SchH. II and SchH. III. Each level consists of training, obedience and protection phases but are progressively more difficult to complete successfully. Training for Schutzhund is intense and must be practised consistently to keep the dog keen. The experience of Schutzhund training is very rewarding for dog and owner, and the Dogue de Bordeaux's tractability is well suited for this type of training.

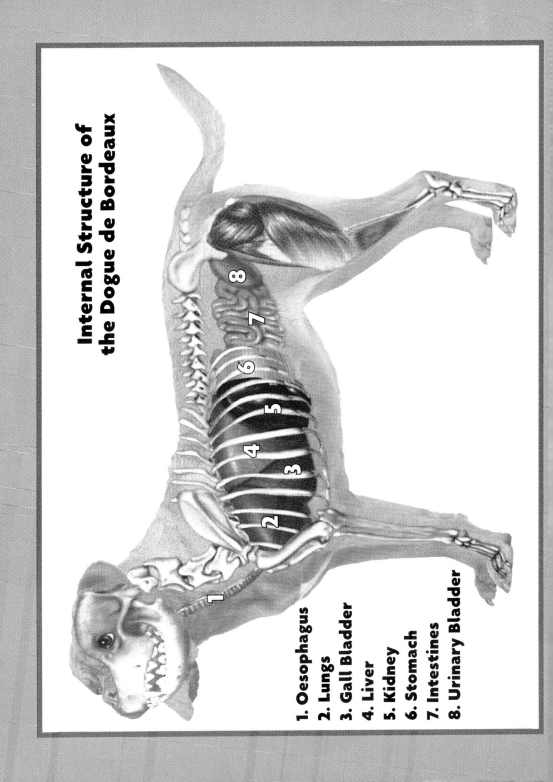

Internal Structure of the Dogue de Bordeaux

1. Oesophagus
2. Lungs
3. Gall Bladder
4. Liver
5. Kidney
6. Stomach
7. Intestines
8. Urinary Bladder

Dogue de Bordeaux

Dogs, being mammals like human beings, suffer many of the same physical illnesses as people. They might even share many of the psychological problems. Since people usually know more about human diseases than canine maladies, many of the terms used in this chapter will be the familiar terms, not necessarily those used by veterinary surgeons. We'll use the term X-RAY, instead of the more accept-able term RADIOGRAPH. We will also use the familiar term SYMPTOMS even though dogs don't have symptoms, which are verbal descriptions of the patient's feelings, dogs have CLINICAL SIGNS. Since dogs can't speak, we have to look for clinical signs...but we will use the term SYMPTOMS in this book.

As a general rule, medicine is PRACTICED. That term is not arbitrary. Medicine is a constantly changing art as we learn more and more about genetics, electronic aids (like CAT scans) and opinions. There are many dog maladies, like canine hip dysplasia, which are not universally treated in the same manner. Some veterinary surgeons opt for surgery more often than others do.

SELECTING A VETERINARY SURGEON

Your selection of a veterinary surgeon should not be based upon personality (as most are) but upon their convenience to your home. You want a doctor who is close as you might have emergencies or multiple visits for treatments. You want a doctor who has services that you might require such as a boarding kennel and grooming facilities, who makes sophisticated pet supplies available and who has a good reputation for ability and responsiveness. There is nothing more frustrating than having to wait a day or more to get a response from a veterinary surgeon.

Before you buy your Dogue de Bordeaux, meet and interview the veterinary surgeons in your area. Take everything into consideration; discuss his background, specialities, fees, emergency policy, etc.

A typical American vet's income categorised according to services performed. This survey dealt with small-animal (pets) practices.

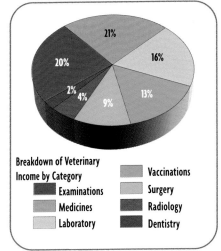

Breakdown of Veterinary Income by Category

- Examinations
- Medicines
- Laboratory
- Vaccinations
- Surgery
- Radiology
- Dentistry

All veterinary surgeons are licensed and their diplomas and/or certificates should be displayed in their waiting rooms. There are, however, many veterinary specialties that usually require further studies and internships. There are specialists in heart problems (veterinary cardiologists), skin problems (veterinary dermatologists), teeth and gum problems (veterinary dentists), eye problems (veterinary ophthalmologists), X-rays (veterinary radiologists), and surgeons who have specialities in bones, muscles or other organs. Most veterinary surgeons do routine surgery such as neutering, stitching up wounds and docking tails for those breeds in which such is required for show purposes. When the problem affecting your dog is serious, it is not unusual or impudent to get another medical opinion, although in Britain you are obliged to advise the vets concerned about this. You might also want to compare costs between several veterinary surgeons. Sophisticated health care and veterinary services can be very costly. Don't be bashful about discussing these costs with your veterinary surgeon or his (her) staff. It is not infrequent that important decisions are based upon financial considerations.

PREVENTATIVE MEDICINE
It is much easier, less costly and more effective to practice preventative medicine than to fight bouts of illness and disease. Properly bred puppies come from parents that were selected based upon their genetic disease profile. Their mothers should have been vaccinated, free of all internal and external parasites, and properly nourished. The dam can pass on disease resistance to her puppies. This resistance can last for eight to ten weeks. She can also pass on parasites and many infections. That's why you should visit the veterinary surgeon who cared for the dam.

WEANING TO FIVE MONTHS OLD
Puppies should be weaned by the time they are about six to eight weeks old. A puppy that remains for ten weeks with its mother and littermates usually adapts better to other dogs and people.

First Aid at a Glance

Burns
Place the affected area under cool water; use ice if only a small area is burnt.

Bee/Insect bites
Apply ice to relieve swelling; antihistamine dosed properly.

Animal bites
Clean any bleeding area; apply pressure until bleeding subsides; go to the vet.

Spider bites
Use cold compress and a pressurised pack to inhibit venom's spreading.

Antifreeze poisoning
Immediately induce vomiting by using hydrogen peroxide.

Fish hooks
Removal best handled by vet; hook must be cut in order to remove.

Snake bites
Pack ice around bite; contact vet quickly; identify snake for proper antivenin.

Car accident
Move dog from roadway with blanket; seek veterinary aid.

Shock
Calm the dog, keep him warm; seek immediate veterinary help.

Nosebleed
Apply cold compress to the nose; apply pressure to any visible abrasion.

Bleeding
Apply pressure above the area; treat wound by applying a cotton pack.

Heat stroke
Submerge dog in cold bath; cool down with fresh air and water; go to the vet.

Frostbite/Hypothermia
Warm the dog with a warm bath, electric blankets or hot water bottles.

Abrasions
Clean the wound and wash out thoroughly with fresh water; apply antiseptic.

Remember: an injured dog may attempt to bite a helping hand from fear and confusion. Always muzzle the dog before trying to offer assistance.

Many people have their newly acquired puppy examined by a veterinary surgeon immediately, which is good idea. The puppy will have its teeth examined, its skeletal conformation checked, and its general health evaluated prior to certification by the veterinary surgeon. Puppies sometimes have problems with their kneecaps, eye cataracts and other eye problems, heart murmurs and undescended testicles. They may also have personality problems and your veterinary surgeon might have training in temperament evaluation.

VACCINATION SCHEDULING

Vaccination programmes usually begin when the puppy is very young. In Britain, some vets give a first vaccination at eight weeks, though most breeders prefer the course to commence at ten weeks so not interfere with the dam's passing of antibodies. Most

> **DID YOU KNOW?**
> Male dogs are neutered. The operation removes the testicles and requires that the dog be anaesthetised. Recovery takes about one week. Females are spayed. This is major surgery and it usually takes a bitch two weeks to recover.

vaccinations are given by injection and should only be done by a veterinary surgeon. Both he and you should keep a record of the date of the injection, the identification of the vaccine and the amount given. Vaccinations should never be given without a 15-day lapse between injections. You must take your vet's advice as to when to vaccinate as this may differ according to the vaccine used. Most vaccinations immunise your puppy against viruses.

The usual vaccines contain immunising doses of several different viruses such as distemper, parvovirus, parainfluenza and hepatitis. There are other vaccines available when the puppy is at risk. You should rely upon professional advice. This is especially true for the booster shot programme. Most vaccination programmes require a booster when the puppy is one year old, and once a year thereafter. In some cases, circumstances may require more frequent immunisa-

> **DID YOU KNOW?**
> Caring for the puppy starts before the puppy is born by keeping the dam healthy and well-nourished. Most puppies have worms, even if they are not evident, so a worming programme is essential. The worms continually shed eggs except during their dormant stage, when they just rest in the tissues of the puppy. During this stage they are not evident during a routine examination.

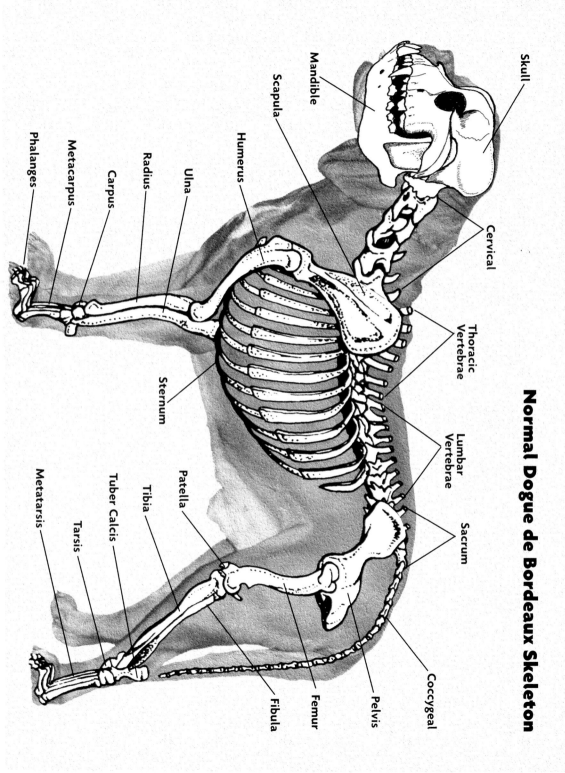

Normal Dogue de Bordeaux Skeleton

Skull

Mandible

Scapula

Cervical

Humerus

Thoracic Vertebrae

Ulna

Radius

Carpus

Lumbar Vertebrae

Metacarpus

Sternum

Phalanges

Sacrum

Patella

Tibia

Tuber Calcis

Tarsis

Metatarsis

Fibula

Femur

Pelvis

Coccygeal

HEALTH AND VACCINATION SCHEDULE

AGE IN WEEKS:	3RD	6TH	8TH	10TH	12TH	14TH	16TH	20-24TH
Worm Control	✔	✔	✔	✔	✔	✔	✔	✔
Neutering								✔
Heartworm*		✔						✔
Parvovirus		✔		✔		✔		✔
Distemper			✔		✔		✔	
Hepatitis			✔		✔		✔	
Leptospirosis		✔		✔		✔		
Parainfluenza		✔		✔		✔		
Dental Examination			✔					✔
Complete Physical			✔					✔
Temperament Testing			✔					
Coronavirus					✔			
Kennel Cough		✔						
Hip Dysplasia							✔	
Rabies*								✔

Vaccinations are not instantly effective. It takes about two weeks for the dog's immunisation system to develop antibodies. Most vaccinations require annual booster shots. Your veterinary surgeon should guide you in this regard.
*Not applicable in the United Kingdom

tions. The effectiveness of a parvovirus vaccination programme can be tested to be certain that the vaccinations are protective by using the parvovirus antibody titer.

DID YOU KNOW?

Not every dog's ears are the same. Ears that are open to the air are healthier than ears with poor air circulation. Sometimes a dog can have two differently shaped ears. You should not probe inside your dog's ears. Only clean that which is accessible with a wad of soft cotton wool.

Kennel cough, more formally known as tracheobronchitis, is treated with a vaccine that is sprayed into the dog's nostrils. Your veterinary surgeon will explain and manage all of these details.

FIVE MONTHS TO ONE YEAR OF AGE

By the time your puppy is five months old, he should have completed his vaccination programme. During his physical examination he should be evaluated for the common hip dysplasia and other diseases of the joints. There are tests to assist in the prediction of these problems.

Unless you intend to breed or show your dog, neutering the puppy at six months of age is recommended. Discuss this with your veterinary surgeon.

By the time your Dogue de Bordeaux is seven or eight months of age, he can be seriously evaluated for his conformation to the club standard to determine show potential and desirability as a sire or dam. If the puppy is not top class and therefore not a candidate for a serious breeding programme, most professionals advise neutering the puppy. Neutering has proven to be extremely beneficial to both male and female puppies. Besides the

DID YOU KNOW?
Vaccines do not work all the time. Sometimes dogs are allergic to them and many times the antibodies, which are supposed to be stimulated by the vaccine, just are not produced. You should keep your dog in the veterinary clinic for an hour after it is vaccinated to be sure there are no allergic reactions.

eliminating the possibility of pregnancy, it inhibits (but does not prevent) breast cancer in bitches and prostate cancer in male dogs.

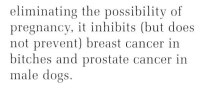

Disease	What is it?	What causes it?	Symptoms
Leptospirosis	Severe disease that affects the internal organs; can be spread to people.	A bacterium, which is often carried by rodents, that enters through mucous membranes and spreads quickly throughout the body.	Range from fever, vomiting and loss of appetite in less severe cases to shock, irreversible kidney damage and possibly death in most severe cases.
Rabies	Potentially deadly virus that infects warm-blooded mammals. Not seen in United Kingdom.	Bite from a carrier of the virus, mainly wild animals.	1st stage: dog exhibits change in behaviour, fear. 2nd stage: dog's behaviour becomes more aggressive. 3rd stage: loss of coordination, trouble with bodily functions.
Parvovirus	Highly contagious virus, potentially deadly.	Ingestion of the virus, which is usually spread through the faeces of infected dogs.	Most common: severe diarrhoea. Also vomiting, fatigue, lack of appetite.
Kennel cough	Contagious respiratory infection.	Combination of types of bacteria and virus. Most common: *Bordetella bronchiseptica* bacteria and parainfluenza virus.	Chronic cough.
Distemper	Disease primarily affecting respiratory and nervous system.	Virus that is related to the human measles virus.	Mild symptoms such as fever, lack of appetite and mucous secretion progress to evidence of brain damage, 'hard pad.'
Hepatitis	Virus primarily affecting the liver.	Canine adenovirus type I (CAV-1). Enters system when dog breathes in particles.	Lesser symptoms include listlessness, diarrhoea, vomiting. More severe symptoms include 'blue-eye' (clumps of virus in eye).
Coronavirus	Virus resulting in digestive problems.	Virus is spread through infected dog's faeces.	Stomach upset evidenced by lack of appetite, vomiting, diarrhoea.

Blood tests are performed for heartworm infestation and it is possible that your puppy will be placed on a preventative therapy that will prevent heartworm infection as well as control other internal parasites.

DOGS OLDER THAN ONE YEAR
Continue to visit the veterinary surgeon at least once a year. There is no such disease as old age, but bodily functions do change with age. The eyes and ears are no longer as efficient nor are the internal workings of the liver, kidneys and intestines. Proper dietary changes, recommended by your veterinary surgeon, can make life more pleasant for the ageing Dogue de Bordeaux and you.

SKIN PROBLEMS IN DOGUES DE BORDEAUX
Veterinary surgeons are consulted by dog owners for skin problems more than any other group of diseases or maladies. Dogs' skin is almost as sensitive as human skin and both suffer almost the same ailments. (Though the occurrence of acne in dogs is rare!) For this reason, veterinary dermatology has developed into a specialty practised by many vets.

Since many skin problems have visual symptoms that are almost identical, it requires the skill of an experienced veterinary dermatologist to identify and cure many of the more severe skin

DID YOU KNOW?
A dental examination is in order when the dog is between six months and one year of age so any permanent teeth that have erupted incorrectly can be corrected. It is important to begin a brushing routine, preferably using a two-sided brushing technique, whereby both sides of the tooth are brushed at the same time. Durable nylon and safe edible chews should be a part of your puppy's arsenal for good health, good teeth and pleasant breath. The vast majority of dogs three to four years old and older has diseases of their gums from lack of dental attention. Using the various types of dental chews can be very effective in controlling dental plaque.

disorders. Pet shops sell many treatments for skin problems but most are directed at symptoms and not the underlying problem(s). If your dog is suffering from a skin disorder, seek professional assistance as quickly as possible. The earlier a disease is identified and treated, the more successful is the cure.

INHERITED SKIN PROBLEMS
Many skin disorders are inherited and some are fatal. Acrodermatitis is an inherited disease that is transmitted by both parents who appear (phenotypically) normal but have

a recessive gene for acrodermatitis, meaning that they carry, but are not affected by the disease.

Acrodermatitis is just one example of how difficult it is to diagnose and treat many dog diseases. The cost and skills required to ascertain whether two dogs should be mated is high even though puppies with acrodermatitis rarely reach two years of age.

Other inherited skin problems are usually not as fatal as acrodermatitis. All inherited diseases must be diagnosed and treated by a veterinary specialist. There are active programmes being undertaken by many veterinary pharmaceutical manufacturers to solve most, if not all, of the common skin problems of dogs.

AUTO-IMMUNE SKIN CONDITIONS

Auto-immune skin conditions are commonly referred to as being allergic to yourself. Allergies, though, usually result in inflammatory reactions to an outside stimulus. Auto-immune diseases cause serious damage to the tissues which are involved.

> **DID YOU KNOW?**
> Feeding your dog properly is very important. An incorrect diet could affect the dog's health, behaviour and nervous system, possibly making a normal dog into an aggressive one.

> **DID YOU KNOW?**
> There is a 25% chance of a puppy getting this fatal gene combination from two parents with recessive genes for acrodermatitis:
>
> AA= NORMAL, HEALTHY
> aa= FATAL
> Aa= RECESSIVE, NORMAL APPEARING
>
> If the female parent has an Aa gene and the male parent has an Aa gene, the chances are one in four that the puppy will have the fatal genetic combination aa.

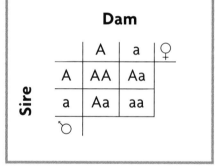

The best known auto-immune disease is lupus. It affects people as well as dogs. The symptoms are very variable and may affect the kidneys, bones, blood chemistry and skin. It can be fatal to both dogs and humans, though it is not thought to be transmissible. It is usually successfully treated with cortisone, prednisone or similar corticosteroid, but extensive use of these drugs can have harmful side effects.

121

Many large breeds of dog are prone to acral lick syndrome. The dog will lick at a spot, usually on one of his front legs, until he has removed all the hair and much of the skin. Your veterinary surgeon can treat the problem, but the cause and the cure are not known.

ACRAL LICK DISEASE

Dogues de Bordeaux and many other dogs have a very poorly understood syndrome called acral lick. The manifestation of the problem is the dog's tireless attack at a specific area of the body, almost always the legs. They lick so intensively that they remove the hair and skin leaving an ugly, large wound. There is no absolute cure, but corticosteroids are the most common treatment.

PARASITE BITES

Many of us are allergic to mosquito bites. The bites itch, erupt and may even become infected. Dogs have the same reaction to fleas, ticks and/or mites. When you feel the prick of the mosquito as it bites you, you have a chance to kill it with your hand. Unfortunately, when our dog is bitten by a flea, tick or mite, it can only scratch it away or bite it. By the time the dog has been bitten, the parasite has done some of its damage. It may also have laid eggs to cause further problems in the near future. The itching from parasite bites is probably due to the saliva injected into the site when the parasite sucks the dog's blood.

AIRBORNE ALLERGIES

Another interesting allergy is pollen allergy. Humans have hay fever, rose fever and other fevers with which they suffer during the pollinating season. Many dogs suffer the same allergies. So when the pollen count is high, your dog might suffer. Don't expect them to sneeze and have runny noses like humans. Dogs react to pollen allergies the same way they react to fleas—they scratch and bite themselves. Dogues de Bordeaux are very susceptible to airborne pollen allergies.

Dogs, like humans, can be tested for allergens. Discuss the testing with your veterinary dermatologist.

FOOD PROBLEMS

FOOD ALLERGIES

Dogs are allergic to many foods that are best-sellers and highly recommended by breeders and veterinary surgeons. Changing the brand of food that you buy may not eliminate the problem because the element of the food to which the dog is allergic may also be contained in the new brand.

Recognising a food allergy is difficult. Humans vomit or have rashes when they eat a food to which they are allergic. Dogs neither vomit nor (usually) develop a rash. Instead they itch, scratch and bite, thus making the diagnosis extremely difficult. While pollen allergies and parasite bites are usually seasonal, food allergies are year-round problems.

Food Intolerance

Food intolerance is the inability of the dog to completely digest certain foods. Puppies that may have done very well on their mother's milk may not do well on cow's milk. Food intolerance may cause loose bowels, passing wind and stomach pains. These are the only obvious symptoms of food intolerance and that makes diagnosis difficult, since these symptoms are often common to other problems as well.

Treating Food Problems

Handling food allergies and food intolerance yourself is possible. Put your dog on a diet that it has never had. Obviously if it has never eaten this new food it can't have been allergic or intolerant of it. Start with a single ingredient that is NOT in the dog's diet at the present time. Ingredients like chopped beef or fish are common in dog's diets, so try something

more exotic like rabbit, pheasant or even just vegetables. Keep the dog on this diet (with no additives) for a month. If the symptoms of food allergy or intolerance disappear, chances are that you have defined the cause.

Don't think that the single ingredient cured the problem. You still must find a suitable diet and ascertain which ingredient in the old diet was objectionable.

> **DID YOU KNOW?**
> Your dog's protein needs are changeable. High activity level, stress, climate and other physical factors may require your dog to have more protein in his diet. Check with your veterinary surgeon.

This is most easily done by adding ingredients to the new diet one at a time until the problem is solved. Let the dog stay on the modified diet for a month before you add another ingredient.

An alternative method is to study the ingredients in the diet to which your dog is allergic or intolerable. Identify the main ingredient in this diet and eliminate it by buying a different food that does not have that ingredient. Keep experimenting until the symptoms disappear after one month on the new diet.

A scanning electron micrograph (S. E. M.) of a dog flea, *Ctenocephalides canis.*

S. E. M. BY DR DENNIS KUNKEL, UNIVERSITY OF HAWAII

EXTERNAL PARASITES

Of all the problems to which dogs are prone, none is more well known and frustrating than fleas. Fleas, which usually refers to fleas, ticks and mites, are relatively simple to cure but difficult to prevent. Parasites that are harboured inside the body are a bit more difficult to cure but they are easier to control.

FLEAS

To control a flea infestation you have to understand its life cycle. Fleas are often thought of as a

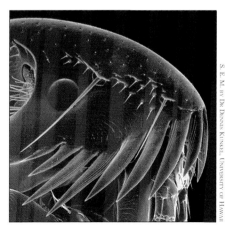

Magnified head of a dog flea, *Ctenocephalides canis.*

S. E. M. BY DR DENNIS KUNKEL, UNIVERSITY OF HAWAII

summertime problem but centrally heated homes have changed the patterns and fleas can be found at any time of the year. Their effective treatment (destruction) is environmental. Unfortunately, no single flea control medicine (insecticide) is effective in every flea infested area. To understand flea control you must apply suitable treatment to the weak link in the life cycle of the flea.

THE LIFE CYCLE OF A FLEA

Fleas are found in four forms: eggs, larvae, pupae and adults. You really need a low-power microscope or hand lens to identify a living flea's eggs, pupae

DID YOU KNOW?

Fleas have been around for millions of years and have adapted to changing host animals.

They are able to go through a complete life cycle in less than one month or they can extend their lives to almost two years by remaining as pupae or cocoons. They do not need blood or any other food for up to 20 months.

They have been measured as being able to jump 300,000 times and can jump 150 times their length in any direction including straight up. Those are just a few of the reasons they are so successful in infesting a dog!

or larva. They spend their whole lives on your Dogue de Bordeaux unless they are forcibly removed by brushing, bathing, scratching or biting.

Several species infest both dog and cats. The dog flea is scientifically known as *Ctenocephalides canis* while the cat flea is *Ctenocephalides felis*. Cat fleas are very common on dogs.

Fleas lay eggs while they are in residence on your dog. These eggs do not adhere to the hair of your dog and they fall off almost as soon as they dry (they may be a bit damp when initially laid). These eggs are the reservoir of future flea infestations. If your dog scratches himself and is able to dislodge a few fleas, they simply fall off and await a future chance to attack a dog...or a person. Yes, fleas from dogs bite people. That's why it is so important to control fleas both on the dog and in the dog's entire environment. You must, therefore, treat the dog and the environment simultaneously.

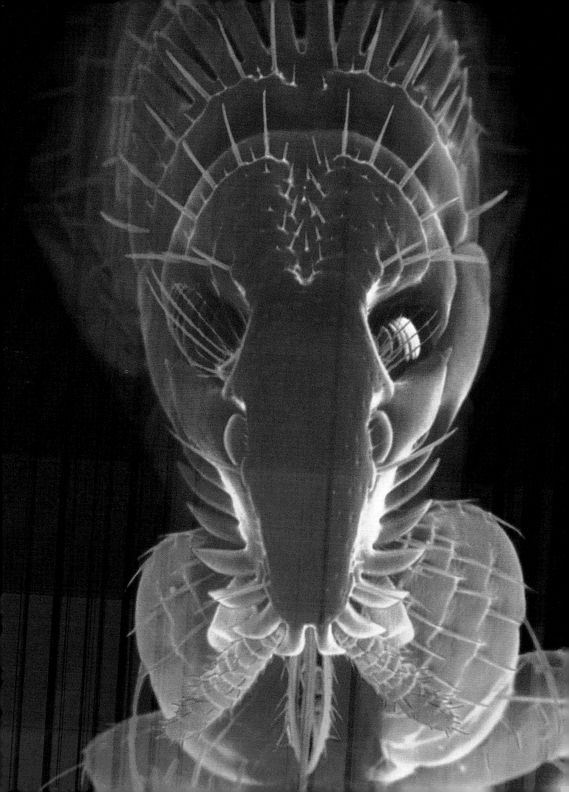

DE-FLEAING THE HOME

Cleanliness is the simple rule. If you have a cat living with your dog, the matter is more complicated since most dog fleas are actually cat fleas. Cats climb onto many areas that are never accessible to dogs (like window sills, table tops, etc.), so you will have to clean all of these areas, too. The hard floor surfaces (tiles, wood, stone and linoleum) must be mopped several times a day. Drops of food onto the floor are actually food for flea larvae! All rugs and furniture must be vacuumed several times a day. Don't forget cupboards, under furniture, cushions. A study has reported that a vacuum cleaner with a beater bar

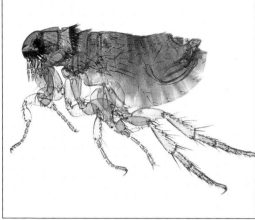

PHOTO BY JEAN CLAUDE REVY/PHOTOTAKE.

A male dog flea, *Ctenocephalides canis.*

DID YOU KNOW?
Never mix flea control products without first consulting your veterinary surgeon. Some products can become toxic when combined with others and can cause serious or fatal consequences.

can remove only 20% of the larvae and 50% of the eggs. The vacuum bags should be discarded into a sealed plastic bag or burned. The vacuum machine itself should be cleaned. The outdoor area to which your dog has access must also be treated with an insecticide.

DID YOU KNOW?
Ivermectin is quickly becoming the drug of choice for treating many parasitic skin diseases in dogs.

For some unknown reason, herding dogs like Collies, Old English Sheepdogs and German Shepherds, etc., are extremely sensitive to ivermectin.

Ivermectin injections have killed some dogs. The ivermectin reaction is a toxicosis which causes tremors, loss of power to move their muscles, prolonged dilatation of the pupil of the eye, coma (unconsciousness), or cessation of breathing (death).

The toxicosis usually starts from 4-6 hours after ingestion or as late as 12 hours. The longer it takes to set in, the milder is the reaction.

Ivermectin should only be prescribed and administered by a vet.

Some ivermectin treatments require two doses.

(FACING PAGE) A scanning electron micrograph of a dog or cat flea, *Ctenocephalides,* magnified more than 100x. This has been colourised for effect.

127

Male cat fleas, *Ctenocephalides felis*, are very commonly found on dogs.

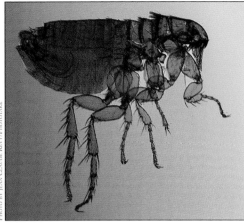

PHOTO BY JEAN CLAUDE REVY/PHOTOTAKE

STERILISING THE ENVIRONMENT

Besides cleaning your home with vacuum cleaners and mops, you have to treat the outdoor range of your dog. This means trimming bushes and spreading insecticide. Be careful not to poison areas in which fishes or other animals reside.

TICKS AND MITES

Though not as common as fleas, ticks and mites are found all over the tropical and temperate world. They don't bite, like fleas; they harpoon. They dig their sharp proboscis (nose) into the dog's skin and drink the blood. Their only food and drink is dog's blood. Dogs can get Lyme disease, Rocky

Your vet will be able to recommend a household insecticidal spray but this must be used with caution, and instructions strictly adhered to.

While there are many drugs available to kill fleas on the dog itself, such as the miracle drug ivermectin, it is best to have the de-fleaing and de-worming supervised by your vet. Ivermectin is effective against many external and internal parasites including heartworms, roundworms, tapeworms, flukes, ticks and mites. It has not been approved for use to control these pests, but veterinary surgeons frequently use it anyway. Ivermectin may not be available in all areas.

Dwight R. Kuhn's magnificent action photo showing a flea jumping from a dog's back.

The Life Cycle of the Flea

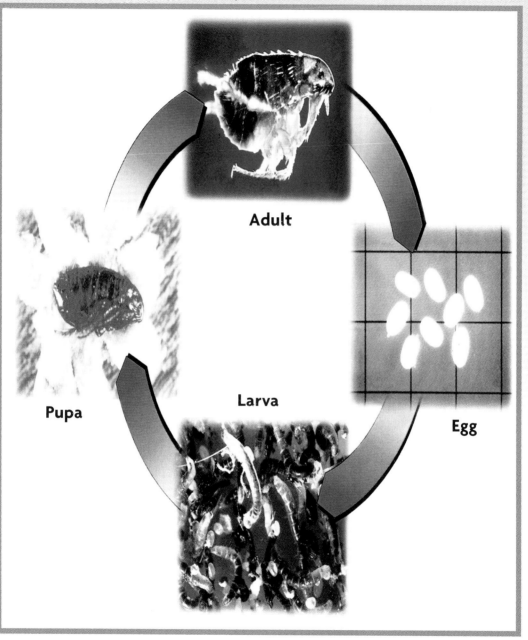

Adult

Pupa

Larva

Egg

The life cycle of the flea was posterised by Fleabusters˙. Poster Courtesy of Fleabusters˙, Rₓ for Fleas.

The eggs of the dog flea. Mountain spotted fever (normally found in the USA only), paralysis and many other diseases from ticks and mites. They may live where fleas are found and they like to hide in cracks or seams in walls wherever dogs live. They are controlled the same way fleas are controlled.

The dog tick, *Dermacentor variabilis*, may well be the most

DID YOU KNOW?

There are drugs which prevent fleas from maturing from egg to adult.

The weak link is the maturation from a larva to a pupa.

Methoprene and fenoxycarb mimic the effect of maturation enhancers, thus, in effect, killing the larva before it pupates.

Methoprene is very effective in killing flea eggs while fenoxycarb is better able to stand UV rays from the sun. There is a combination of both drugs which has an effective life of 6 months and destroys 93% of the flea population.

It is important, in order to effectively control fleas, that you use products designed to kill fleas at all stages of growth, Manufacturers make such products, which are specifically designed for this purpose, and specially made to be safe for use in the home and on the dog.

DID YOU KNOW?

Never allow your dog to swim in polluted water or public areas where water quality can be suspect. Even perfectly clear water can harbour parasites, many of which can cause serious to fatal illnesses in canines. Areas inhabited by waterfowl and other wildlife are especially dangerous.

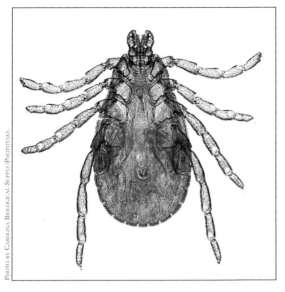

mange. Some are contagious, like *Cheyletiella*, ear mites, scabies and chiggers. The non-contagious mites are *Demodex*. The most serious of the mites is the ear mite infestation. Ear mites are usually controlled with ivermectin.

It is essential that your dog be treated for mange as quickly as possible because some forms of mange are transmissible to people.

A brown dog tick, *Rhipicephalus sanguineus*, is an uncommon but annoying tick found on dogs.

common dog tick in many geographical areas, especially those areas where the climate is hot and humid.

Most dog ticks have life expectancies of a week to six months, depending upon climatic conditions. They can neither jump nor fly, but they can crawl slowly and can range up to 5 metres (16 feet) to reach a sleeping or unsuspecting dog.

MANGE

Mites cause a skin irritation called

Human lice look like dog lice; the two are closely related.

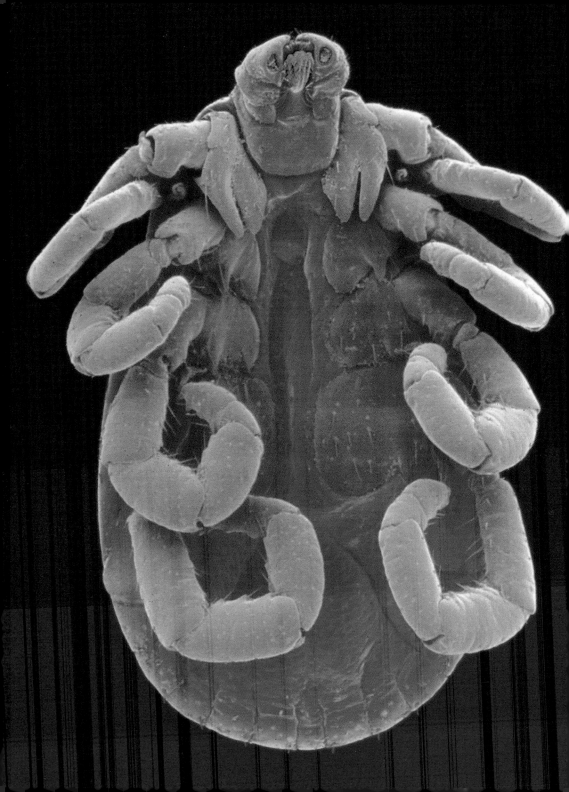

A deer tick, the carrier of Lyme disease.

Photo by Dr. Andrew Spielman/Phototake

(FACING PAGE)
The dog tick, *Dermacentor variabilis*, is probably the most common tick found on dogs. Look at the strength in its eight legs! No wonder it's hard to detach them.

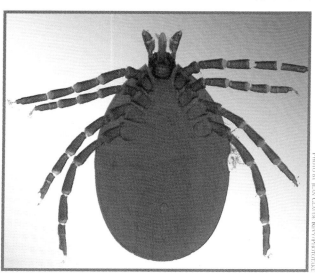

An uncommon dog tick of the genus *Ixode*. Magnified 10x.

Photo by Jean Claude Revy/Phototake

Two views of the mange mite, *Psoroptes bovis.*

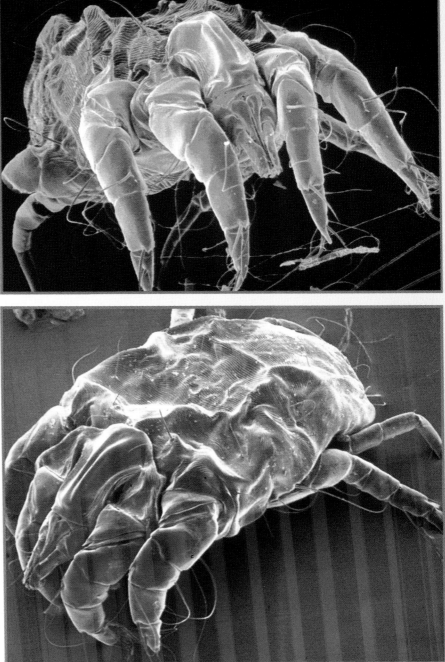

SEM by James Hayden-Yoav/Phototake

SEM by James Hayden-Yoav/Phototake

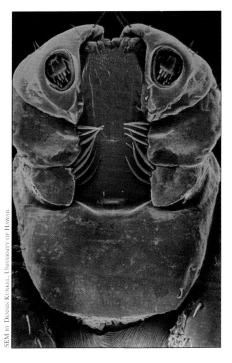

SEM by Dennis Kunkel, University of Hawaii

INTERNAL PARASITES

Most animals—fishes, birds and mammals, including dogs and humans—have worms and other parasites that live inside their bodies. According to Dr. Herbert R. Axelrod, the fish pathologist, there are two kinds of parasites: dumb and smart. The smart parasites live in peaceful cooperation with their hosts (symbiosis), while the dumb parasites kill their host. Most of the worm infections are relatively easy to control. If they are not controlled they eventually weaken the host dog to the point that other medical problems occur, but they are not dumb parasites.

ROUNDWORMS

The roundworms that infect dogs are scientifically known as *Toxocara canis*. They live in the dog's intestine. The worms shed eggs continually. It has been estimated that a Dogue de Bordeaux produces about 150 grammes of faeces every day. Each gramme of faeces averages 10,000–12,000 eggs of roundworms. There are no known areas in which dogs roam that do not contain roundworm eggs. The greatest danger of roundworms is that they infect

The head of the dog tick, *Dermacentor variabilis.*

DID YOU KNOW?

Ridding your puppy of worms is VERY IMPORTANT because certain worms that puppies carry, such as tapeworms and roundworms, can infect humans.

Breeders initiate a deworming programme at or about four weeks of age. The routine is repeated every two or three weeks until the puppy is three months old. The breeder from whom you obtained your puppy should provide you with the complete details of the deworming programme.

Your veterinary surgeon can prescribe and monitor the programme of deworming for you. The usual programme is treating the puppy every 15 to 20 days until the puppy is positively worm free.

It is not advised that you treat your puppy with drugs that are not recommended professionally.

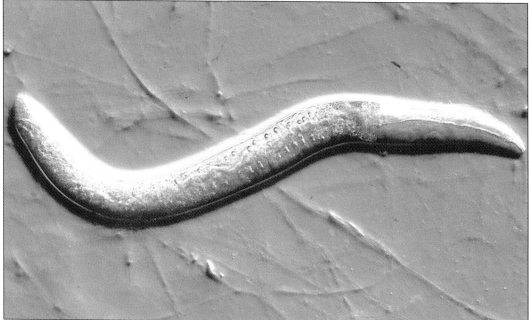

Two views of the roundworm, *Rhabditis*. The roundworm can infect both dogs and humans.

people, too! It is wise to have your dog tested regularly for roundworms.

Pigs also have roundworm infections that can be passed to human and dogs. The typical roundworm parasite is called *Ascaris lumbricoides*.

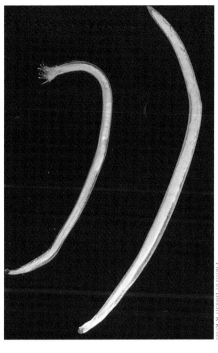

Male and female hookworms, *Ancylostoma caninum*, are uncommonly found in pet or show dogs in Britain. Hookworms may infect other dogs that have exposure to grasslands.

PHOTO BY DWIGHT R KUHN

DID YOU KNOW?

Humans, rats, squirrels, foxes, coyotes, wolves, mixed breeds of dogs and purebred dogs are all susceptible to tapeworm infection. Except in humans, tapeworms are usually not a fatal infection. Infected individuals can harbour a thousand parasitic worms. Tapeworms have two sexes—male and female (many other worms have only one sex—male and female in the same worm). If dogs eat infected rats or mice, they get the tapeworm disease.

One month after attaching to a dog's intestine, the worm starts shedding eggs. These eggs are infective immediately. Infective eggs can live for a few months without a host animal. Roundworms, whipworms and tapeworms are just a few of the other commonly known worms that infect dogs.

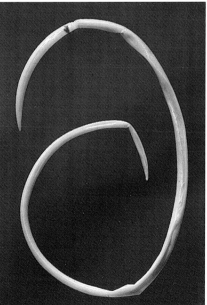

The roundworm *Rhabditis*.

PHOTO BY CAROLINA BIOLOGICAL SUPPLY/PHOTOTAKE

137

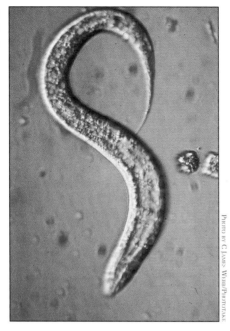

The infective stage of the hookworm larva.

PHOTO BY C. JAMES WEBB/PHOTOTAKE

HOOKWORMS

The worm *Ancylostoma caninum* is commonly called the dog hookworm. It is dangerous to humans and cats. It also has teeth by which it attaches itself to the intestines of the dog. It changes the site of its attachment about six times a day and the dog loses blood from each detachment, possibly causing iron-deficiency anaemia. They are easily purged from the dog with many medications, the best of which seems to be ivermectin even though it has not been approved for such use.

In Britain the 'temperate climate' hookworm (*Uncinaria stenocephala*) is rarely found in

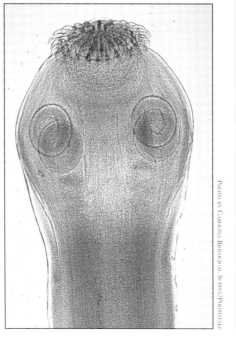

The head and rostellum (the round prominence on the scolex) of a tapeworm, which infects dogs and humans.

PHOTO BY CAROLINA BIOLOGICAL SUPPLY/PHOTOTAKE

DID YOU KNOW?

Average size dogs can pass 1,360,000 roundworm eggs every day.

For example, if there were only 1 million dogs in the world, the world would be saturated with 1,300 metric tonnes of dog faeces. These faeces would contain 15,000,000,000 roundworm eggs.

7 to 31 percent of home gardens and children's play boxes in the U. S. contained roundworm eggs.

Flushing dog's faeces down the toilet is not a safe practice because the usual sewage treatments do not destroy roundworm eggs.

Infected puppies start shedding roundworm eggs at 3 weeks of age. They can be infected by their mother's milk.

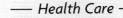

pet or show dogs, but can occur in hunting packs, racing Greyhounds and sheepdogs because the worms can be prevalent wherever dogs are exercised regularly on grassland.

TAPEWORMS

There are many species of tapeworms. They are carried by fleas! The dog eats the flea and starts the tapeworm cycle. Humans can also be infected with tapeworms, so don't eat fleas! Fleas are so small that your dog could pass them onto your hands, your plate or your food and thus make it possible for you to ingest a flea which is carrying tapeworm eggs.

While tapeworm infection is not life threatening in dogs (smart parasite!), it can be the cause of a very serious liver disease for humans. About 50 percent of the humans infected with *Echinococcus multilocularis*, a type of tapeworm that causes alveolar hydatis, perish.

HEARTWORMS

Heartworms are thin, extended worms up to 30 cms (12 ins) long which live in a dog's heart and the major blood vessels surrounding it. Dogues de Bordeaux may have up to 200 of these worms. The symptoms may be loss of energy, loss of appetite, coughing, the development of a pot belly and anaemia.

> **DID YOU KNOW?**
> You are your dog's caretaker and his dentist. Vets warn that plaque and tartar buildup on the teeth will damage the gums and allow bacteria to enter the dog's bloodstream, causing serious damage to the animal's vital organs. Studies show that over 50 percent of dogs have some form of gum disease before age three. Daily or weekly tooth cleaning (with a brush or soft gauze pad wipes) can add years to your dog's life.

Heartworms are transmitted by mosquitoes. The mosquito drinks the blood of an infected dog and takes in larvae with the blood. The larvae, called microfilaria, develop within the body of the mosquito and are passed on to the next dog bitten after the larvae mature. It takes two to three weeks for the larvae to develop to the infective stage within the body of the mosquito. Dogs should be treated at about six weeks of age, then every six months.

Blood testing for heartworms is not necessarily indicative of how seriously your dog is infected. This is a dangerous disease. Although heartworm is a problem for dogs in America, Australia, Asia and Central Europe, dogs in the United Kingdom are not affected by heartworm.

139

The heartworm, *Dirofilaria immitis.*

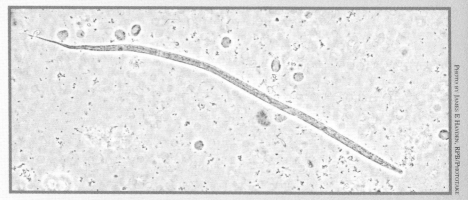

Photo by James E Hayden, RPB/Phototake

Magnified heartworm larvae, *Dirofilaria immitis.*

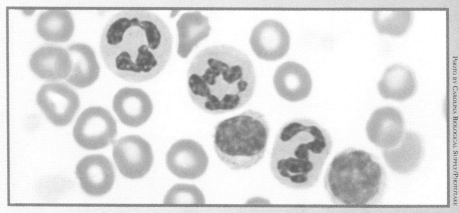

Photo by Carolina Biological Supply/Phototake

The heart of a dog infected with canine heartworm, *Dirofilaria immitis.*

Photo by James E Hayden, RPB/Phototake

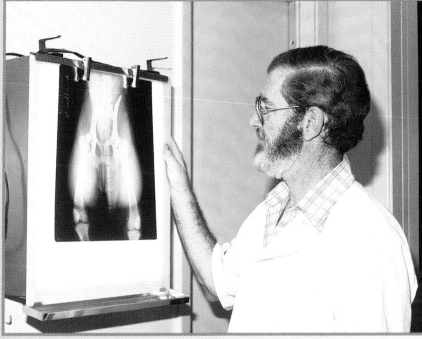

(Above) A veterinary surgeon evaluating a dog's x-ray for hip dysplasia. Diagnosis can only be made using radiographic techniques, which are interpreted (read) by a suitably trained veterinary surgeon.

(Below) The lateral (far left illustration) and flexed lateral (far right illustration) of a three-year-old dog's elbow manifesting elbow dysplasia with associated problems (acute, severe weight-bearing lameness of the right forelimb).

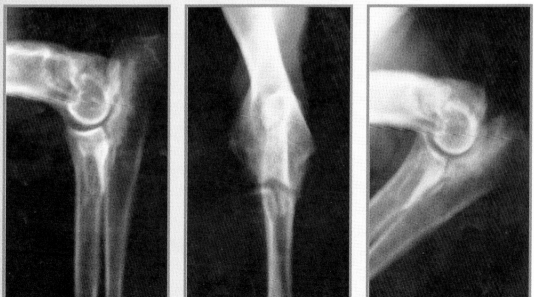

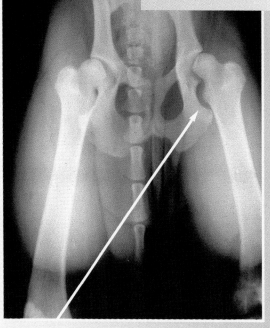

DO YOU KNOW ABOUT HIP DYSPLASIA?

Hip dysplasia is a fairly common condition found in purebred dogs. When a dog has hip dysplasia, its hind leg has an incorrectly formed hip joint. By constant use of the hip joint, it becomes more and more loose, wears abnormally and may become arthritic.

Hip dysplasia can only be confirmed with an x-ray, but certain symptoms may indicate a problem. Your dog may have a hip dysplasia problem if it walks in a peculiar manner, hops instead of smoothly runs, uses his hind legs in unison (to keep the pressure off the weak joint), has trouble getting up from a prone position or always sits with both legs together on one side of its body.

As the dog matures, it may adapt well to life with a bad hip, but in a few years the arthritis develops and many dogs with hip dysplasia become cripples.

Hip dysplasia is considered an inherited disease and can usually be diagnosed when the dog is three to nine months old. Some experts claim that a special diet might help your puppy outgrow the bad hip, but the usual treatments are surgical. The removal of the pectineus muscle, the removal of the round part of the femur, reconstructing the pelvis and replacing the hip with an artificial one are all surgical interventions that are expensive, but they are usually very successful. Follow the advice of your veterinary surgeon.

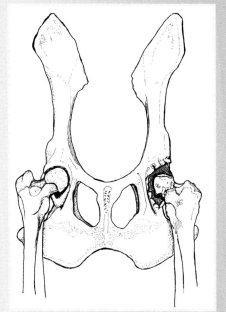

Hip dysplasia is a badly worn hip joint caused by improper fit of the bone into the socket. It is easily the most common hip problem in Dogue de Bordeaux. (Below) The healthy hip joint on the left and the unhealthy hip joint on the right.

CDS: COGNITIVE DYSFUNCTION SYNDROME
"Old-Dog Syndrome"

There are many ways to evaluate old-dog syndrome. Veterinary surgeons have defined CDS (cognitive dysfunction syndrome) as the gradual deterioration of cognitive abilities. These are indicated by changes in the dog's behaviour. When a dog changes its routine response, and maladies have been eliminated as the cause of these behavioural changes, then CDS is the usual diagnosis.

More than half the dogs over 8 years old suffer some form of CDS. The older the dog, the more chance it has of suffering from CDS. In humans, doctors often dismiss the CDS behavioural changes as part of 'winding down.'

There are four major signs of CDS: frequent toilet accidents inside the home, sleeps much more or much less than normal, acts confused, and fails to respond to social stimuli.

SYMPTOMS OF CDS

FREQUENT TOILET ACCIDENTS
- *Urinates in the house.*
- *Defecates in the house.*
- *Doesn't signal that he wants to go out.*

SLEEP PATTERNS
- *Moves much more slowly.*
- *Sleeps more than normal during the day.*
- *Sleeps less during the night.*
- *Walks around listlessly and without a destination goal.*

CONFUSION
- *Goes outside and just stands there.*
- *Appears confused with a faraway look in his eyes.*
- *Hides more often.*
- *Doesn't recognise friends.*
- *Doesn't come when called.*

FAILS TO RESPOND TO SOCIAL STIMULI
- *Comes to people less frequently, whether called or not.*
- *Doesn't tolerate petting for more than a short time.*
- *Doesn't come to the door when you return home from work.*

Dogue de Bordeaux

The term old is a qualitative term. For dogs, as well as their masters, old is relative. Certainly we can all distinguish between a puppy Dogue de Bordeaux and an adult Dogue de Bordeaux—there are the obvious physical traits such as size, appearance, and facial expression as well as personality traits and puppy antics. Puppies that are nasty are very rare. Puppies and young dogs like to play with children. Children's natural exuberance is a good match for the seemingly endless energy of young dogs who like to run, jump, chase and retrieve. When dogs grow up and cease their interaction with children, they are often thought of as being too old to play with the kids.

On the other hand, if a Dogue de Bordeaux is only exposed to people over 60 years of age, its life will normally be less active and it will not seem to be getting old as soon as its activity level slows down.

If people live to be 100 years old, dogs live to be 20 years old. While this is a good rule of thumb, it is VERY inaccurate. When trying to compare dog years to human years, you cannot make a generalisation about all dogs. You can make the generalisation that 10 years is a good life span for a Dogue de Bordeaux, but you cannot compare it to that of a Chihuahua, as many small breeds typically live longer than large breeds. Dogs are generally considered mature within three years. They can reproduce even earlier. The first three years of a dog's life are more like seven times that of comparable humans. That means a 3-year-old dog is like a 21-year-old person. As the curve of comparison shows, there is no hard and fast rule for comparing dog and human ages. The comparison is made even more difficult, for not all humans age at the same rate...and human females live longer than human males.

DID YOU KNOW?

The bottom line is simply that a dog is getting old when YOU think it is getting old because it slows down in its general activities, including walking, running, eating, jumping and retrieving. On the other hand, certain activities increase, like more sleeping, more barking and more repetition of habits like going to the door when you put your coat on without being called.

When Your Dogue de Bordeaux Gets Old

Signs the Owner Can Look For

IF YOU NOTICE...	IT COULD INDICATE...
Discolouration of teeth and gums, foul breath, loss of appetite	Abcesses, gum disease, mouth lesions
Lumps, bumps, cysts, warts, fatty tumours	Cancers, benign or malignant
Cloudiness of eyes, apparent loss of sight.	Cataracts, lenticular sclerosis, PRA, retinal dysplasia, blindness
Flaky coat, alopaecia (hair loss)	Hormonal problems, hypothyroidism
Obesity, appetite loss, excessive weight gain	Various problems
Household accidents, increased urination	Diabetes, kidney or bladder disease
Increased thirst	Kidney disease, diabetes mellitus
Change in sleeping habits, coughing	Heart disease
Difficulty moving	Arthritis, degenerative joint disease, spondylosis (degenerative spine disease)

If you notice any of these signs, an appointment should be made immediately with a veterinary surgeon for a thorough evaluation.

DID YOU KNOW?

Your senior dog may lose interest in eating, not because he's less hungry but because his senses of smell and taste have diminished. The old chow simply does not smell as good as it once did. Additionally, older dogs use less energy and thereby can sustain themselves on less food.

WHAT TO LOOK FOR IN SENIORS

Most veterinary surgeons and behaviourists use the seventh year mark as the time to consider a dog a 'senior.' The term 'senior' does not imply that the dog is geriatric and has begun to fail in mind and body. Ageing is essentially a slowing process. Humans readily admit that they feel a difference in their activity level from age 20 to 30, and then from 30 to 40, etc. By treating the seven-year-old dog as a senior, owners are able to implement certain therapeutic and preventive medical strategies with the help of their veterinary surgeons. A senior-care

DID YOU KNOW?

An old dog starts to show one or more of the following symptoms:

• The hair on its face and paws starts to turn grey. The colour breakdown usually starts around the eyes and mouth.

• Sleep patterns are deeper and longer and the old dog is harder to awaken.

• Food intake diminishes.

• Responses to calls, whistles and other signals are ignored more and more.

• Eye contacts do not evoke tail wagging (assuming they once did).

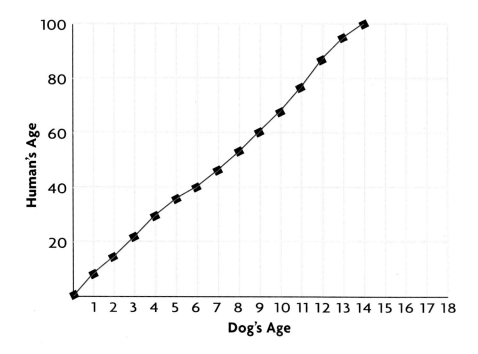

programme should include at least two veterinary visits per year, screening sessions to determine the dog's health status, as well as nutritional counselling. Veterinary surgeons determine the senior dog's health status through a blood smear for a complete blood count, serum chemistry profile with electrolytes, urinalysis, blood pressure check, electrocardiogram, ocular tonometry (pressure on the eyeball), and dental prophylaxis.

Such an extensive programme for senior dogs is well advised before owners start to see the obvious physical signs of ageing, such as slower and inhibited movement, greying, increased sleep/nap periods, and disinterest in play and other activity. This preventative programme promises a longer, healthier life for the ageing dog. Amongst the physical problems common in ageing dogs are the loss of sight and vision, arthritis, kidney and liver failure, diabetes mellitus, heart disease, and Cushing's disease (a hormonal disease).

In addition to the physical manifestations discussed, there are some behavioural changes and problems related to ageing dogs. Dogs suffering from hearing or vision loss, dental discomfort or arthritis can become aggressive. Likewise the near-deaf and/or blind dog may be startled more easily and react in an unexpected-ly aggressive manner. Seniors suffering from senility can become more impatient and irritable. Housesoiling accidents are associated with loss of mobility, kidney problems, loss of sphincter control as well as plaque accumulation, physiological brain changes, and reactions to medications. Older dogs, just like young puppies, suffer from separation anxiety, which can lead to

DID YOU KNOW?

The symptoms listed below are symptoms that gradually appear and become more noticeable. They are not life threatening, however, the symptoms below are to be taken very seriously and a discussion with your veterinary surgeon is warranted:

• Your dog cries and whimpers when it moves and stops running completely.

• Convulsions start or become more serious and frequent. The usual convulsion (spasm) is when the dog stiffens and starts to tremble being unable or unwilling to move. The seizure usually lasts for 5 to 30 minutes.

• Your dog drinks more water and urinates more frequently. Wetting and bowel accidents take place indoors without warning.

• Vomiting becomes more and more frequent.

excessive barking, whining, housesoiling, and destructive behaviour. Seniors may become fearful of everyday sounds, such as vacuum cleaners, heaters, thunder, and passing traffic. Some dogs have difficulty sleeping, due to discomfort, the need for frequent potty visits, and the like. Owners should avoid spoiling the older dog with too many fatty treats. Obesity is a common problem in older dogs and subtracts years from their lifespan. Keep the senior dog as trim as possible since excessive weight puts additional stress on the body's vital organs. Some breeders recommend supplementing the diet with foods high in fibre and lower in calories. Adding fresh vegetables and marrow broth to the senior's diet makes a tasty, low-calorie, low-fat supplement. Vets also offer specialty diets for senior dogs that are worth exploring.

Your dog, as he nears his twilight years, needs his owner's patience and good care more than ever. Never punish an older dog for an accident or abnormal behaviour. For all the years of love, protection and companionship that your dog has provided, he deserves special attention and courtesies. The older dog may need to relieve himself at 3 a.m. because he can no longer hold it for eight hours. Older dogs may not be able to remain crated for more than two or three hours. It may be time to give up a sofa or chair to your old friend. Although he may not seem as enthusiastic about your attention and petting, he does appreciate the considerations you offer as he gets older.

Your Bordeaux does not understand why his world is slowing down. Owners must make the transition into the golden years as pleasant and rewarding as possible.

WHAT TO DO WHEN THE TIME COMES

You are never fully prepared to make a rational decision about putting your dog to sleep. It is very obvious that you love your Dogue de Bordeaux or you would not be reading this book. Putting a loved dog to sleep is extremely difficult. It is a decision that must be made with your veterinary surgeon. You are usually forced to make the decision when one of the life-threatening symptoms listed above becomes serious enough for you to seek medical (veterinary) help.

DID YOU KNOW?

Euthanasia must be done by a licensed veterinary surgeon. There also may be societies for the prevention of cruelty to animals in your area. They often offer this service upon a vet's recommendation.

Pet cemeteries are to be found throughout the world. Your veterinary surgeon usually can assist you in locating a pet cemetery where you can memorialise your dog.

If the prognosis of the malady indicates the end is near and your beloved pet will only suffer more and experience no enjoyment for the balance of its life, then there euthanasia is the right choice.

WHAT IS EUTHANASIA?
Euthanasia derives from the Greek meaning good death. It means the planned, painless killing of a dog suffering from a painful, incurable condition, or who is so aged that it cannot walk, see, eat or control its excretory functions.

Euthanasia is usually accomplished by injection with an overdose of an anaesthesia or barbiturate. Aside from the prick of the needle, the experience is usually painless.

HOW ABOUT YOU?
The days during which the dog becomes ill and the end occurs can be unusually stressful for you. Usually your dog can be maintained on drugs for a few days while it is kept in the clinic in order to give you ample time to make a decision. If you are the head of the family and have children, you should involve them in the decision of putting your Dogue de Bordeaux to sleep. Both the decision making process and euthanasia itself are painful and stressful for the family of the dog.

If this is your first experience with the death of a loved one, you may need the comfort dictated by your religious beliefs. Talking

149

with members of the family or people who have lived through this same experience, can ease the burden of your inevitable decision...but then what?

There are facilities at most pet cemeteries in which you can keep your pet's ashes after cremation.

THE FINAL RESTING PLACE?

Dogs can have some of the same privileges as humans. They can occasionally be buried in their entirety in a pet cemetery which is generally expensive, or if they have died at home can be buried in your garden in a place suitably marked with some stone or newly planted tree or bush. Alternatively they can be cremated and the ashes returned to you, or some people prefer to leave their dogs at the surgery for the vet to dispose of.

All of these options should be discussed frankly and openly with your veterinary surgeon. Do not be afraid to ask financial questions. Cremations can be individual, but a less expensive option is mass cremation, although of course the ashes can

not then be returned. Vets can usually arrange cremation services on your behalf, but you must be aware that in Britain if your dog has died at the surgery the vet cannot legally allow you to take your dog's body home.

GETTING ANOTHER DOG?

The grief of losing your beloved dog will be as lasting as the grief of losing a human friend or relative. You cannot go out and buy another grandfather, but you can go out and buy another Dogue de Bordeaux. In most cases, if your dog died of old age (if there is such a thing), it had slowed down considerably. Do you want a new Dogue de Bordeaux puppy or perhaps you would prefer a different breed to avoid direct comparison.

Most people usually buy the same breed they had before because they know (and love) the characteristics of that breed. Then, too, they often know people who have the same breed and perhaps they are lucky enough that one of their friends expects a litter soon. What could be better?

> **DID YOU KNOW?**
> The more open discussion you have about the whole stressful occurrence, the easier it will be for you when the time comes.

Is the puppy you selected growing into a handsome representative of his breed? You are rightly proud of your handsome little tyke, and he has mastered nearly all of the basic obedience commands that you have taught him. How about attending a dog show and seeing how the other half of the dog-loving world lives! Even if you never imagined yourself standing in the centre ring at the Crufts Dog Show, why not dream a little?

The first concept that the canine novice learns when watching a dog show is that each dog first competes against members of its own breed, provided that the show is judged on the Group system. Once the judge has selected the best member of each breed, that chosen dog will then compete with other dogs in its group. Finally the best of each group will compete for Best in Show and Reserve Best in Show.

The second concept that you must understand is that the dogs are not actually competing with one another. The judge compares each dog against the breed standard, which is a written description of the ideal specimen of the breed. Although some breed standards were based on an existing dog, most

breeders bemoan that the perfect dog (as described in the breed standard) never walked into a show ring, has never been bred and, to the woe of dog breeders around the globe, does not exist. With every litter, breeders attempt to get close to this ideal, but theoretically the 'perfect' dog is so elusive that it is impossible to produce. (Even if the 'perfect' dog were born, breeders and judges would never agree that it was indeed 'perfect.')

DID YOU KNOW?

You can get information about dog shows from kennel clubs and breed clubs:

Fédération Cynologique Internationale
14, rue Leopold II, B-6530 Thuin, Belgium
www.fci.be

The Kennel Club
1-5 Clarges St.,
Piccadilly, London W1Y 8AB, UK
www.the-kennel-club.org.uk

American Kennel Club
5580 Centerview Dr.,
Raleigh, NC 27606-3390, USA
www.akc.org

Canadian Kennel Club
89 Skyway Ave., Suite 100, Etobicoke, Ontario
M9W 6R4 Canada
www.ckc.ca

If you are interested in exploring dog shows, your best bet is to join your local breed club, or if no local club exists to join the breed's national club. These clubs often host shows (often matches and open shows for beginners), send out newsletters, offer training days and provide an outlet to meet members who are often friendly and generous with their advice and contacts. To locate the nearest breed club for you, contact The Kennel Club, the ruling body for the British dog world. The Kennel Club can also provide information on conformation shows, working trials, obedience trials, agility trials and field trials. The Kennel Club furnishes the rules and regulations for all these events plus general dog registration and other basic requirements

of dog ownership. Its annual show, held in Birmingham, is the largest bench show in England. Every year no fewer than 20,000 of the UK's best dogs qualify to participate in a marvellous show lasting four days.

There are different kinds of shows held under the auspices of The Kennel Club, which governs shows in Great Britain, Australia, South Africa and beyond. At the most competitive and prestigious of these shows, the Championship Shows, a dog can earn Challenge Certificates (CC), and thereby become a 'champion.' A dog must earn three Challenge Certificates under three different judges to earn the prefix of 'Sh Ch' or 'Ch' Note that some breeds must qualify in a field trial in order to gain the title of full Champion. Challenge Certificates are awarded to a very small percentage of the dogs competing, especially as in Britain dogs that are already Champions also compete for these coveted CCs. The number of Challenge Certificates awarded in any one year is based upon the total number of dogs in each breed entered for competition. There three types of Championship Shows, an all-breed General Championship Show for all Kennel Club-recognised breeds, a Group Championship Show, limited to breeds within on of the country's

Although the Dogue is not a typical agility trial contender, with proper training and precautions, the breed can excel in this venue as well.

Dogues de Bordeaux in the breed ring. The judge compares the dogs not to each other, but rather to the requirements detailed in the breed standard.

seven groups, and a Breed Show, usually confined to a single breed.

Open Shows are generally less competitive and are frequently used as 'practice shows' for young dogs. These shows, of which there are hundreds each year, can be invitingly social events and are great first show experiences for the novice. If you're just considering watching a show to wet your paws, an Open Show is a great choice.

While Championship and Open Shows are most important for the beginner to understand, there are other types of shows in which the interested dog owner can participate. Training clubs, for example, sponsor Matches that can be entered on the day of the show for a nominal fee. In introductory level exhibitions two dogs are pulled out of a hat and 'matched.' The winner of that match goes on to the next round, and eventually only one dog is left undefeated.

Exemption Shows are much more light-hearted affairs with usually only four pedigree classes and several 'fun' classes, all of which can be entered on the day. The proceeds of and Exemption Show must be given to a charity and are sometimes held in conjunction with small agricultural shows. Limited Shows are also available in small number, but entry is restricted to members of the club which hosts the show, although one can usually join the club when making an entry.

Before you actually step into the ring, you would be well advised to sit back and observe the judge's ring procedure. If it is your first time in the ring, do not be over-anxious and run to the front of the line. It is much better to stand back and study how the exhibitor in front of you is performing. The judge asks each handler to 'stand' the dog, hopefully showing the dog off to his best advantage. The judge will observe the dog from a distance and from different angles, approach the dog, check his teeth, overall structure, alertness and muscle tone, as well as consider how well the dog 'conforms' to the standard. Most importantly, the judge will have the exhibitor move the dog around the ring in some pattern that he or she should specify (another advantage to not going first, but always listen since some judges change their directions, and the judge is always right!) Finally the judge will give the dog one last look before moving on to the next exhibitor.

If you are not in the top three at your first show, do not be discouraged. Be patient and consistent and you may eventual-ly find yourself in the winning lineup. Remember that the winners were once in your shoes and have devoted many hours and much money to earn the placement. If you find that your dog is losing every time and never getting a nod, it may be time to consider a different dog sport or just to enjoy your Dogue de Bordeaux as a pet.

FÉDÉRATION CYNOLOGIQUE INTERNATIONALE
Established in 1911, the Fédération Cynologique

DID YOU KNOW?

The FCI is divided into ten 'Groups.' At the World Dog Show, the following 'Classes' are offered for each breed: Puppy Class (6–9 months), Youth Class (9–18 months), Open Class (15 months or older) and Champion Class. A dog can be awarded a classification of Excellent, Very Good, Good, Sufficient and Not Sufficient. Puppies can be awarded classifications of Very Promising, Promising or Not Promising. Four placements are made in each class. After all sexes and classes are judged, a Best of Breed is selected. Other special groups and classes may also be shown. Each exhibitor showing a dog receives a written evaluation from the judge.

Besides the World Dog Show, you can exhibit your dog at speciality shows held by different breed clubs. Speciality shows may have their own regulations.

The judge examines carefully and pays close attention to the unique head and undershot bite of the Dogue de Bordeaux.

(Inset) Precise specifications are set forth for the Dogue's undershot bite—the upper jaw must extend beyond the upper jaw by 0.5 to 2.0 cms (1/5 to 3/4 inch). The puppy's bite, of course, will not reach these specifications until maturity.

Internationale represents the 'world kennel club,' the international body brings uniformity to the breeding, judging and showing of purebred dogs. The FCI originally included only four European nations: France, Holland, Austria and Belgium (which remains its headquarters). Today the organisation embraces nations on six continents and recognises well over 300 breeds of purebred dog. There are three titles attainable through the FCI: the International Champion, which is the most prestigious; the International Beauty Champion, which is based on aptitude certificates in different countries and the International Trial Champion, which is based on achievement in obedience trials in different countries. Quarantine laws in England and Australia prohibit most exhibitors from entering FCI shows. The rest of the European Nation does participate in these impressive canine spectacles, the largest of which is the World Dog Show, hosted in a different country each year. FCI sponsors both national and international shows. The hosting country determines the judging system and breed standards are always based on the breed's country of origin.

155

INDEX

Page numbers in **boldface** indicate illustrations.

My Dogue de Bordeaux

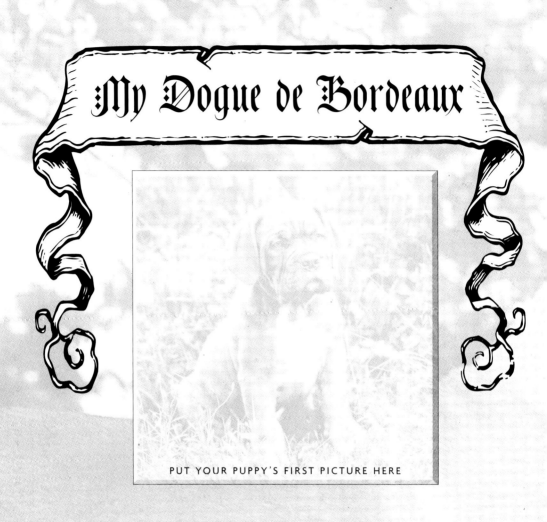

PUT YOUR PUPPY'S FIRST PICTURE HERE

Dog's Name _____

Date _____ Photographer _____